GILL NICHOLLS

PROFESSIONAL
DEVELOPMENT
(in) *Higher Education*

new dimensions & directions

**KOGAN
PAGE**

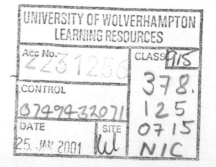

First published in 2001

Kogan Page Limited
120 Pentonville Road
London N1 9JN
UK

Stylus Publications Inc
22883 Quicksilver Drive
Sterling VA 20166-2012
USA

British Library Cataloguing in Publication Data

A CIP record for this book is available from the British Library.

ISBN 0 7494 3207 1

Typeset by Kogan Page
Printed and bound in Great Britain by Clays Ltd, St Ives plc

Contents

Preface

What might we understand by a book carrying the title *Professional Development in Higher Education*? On the face of it, it might seem a little odd, for the academic community has been around for some 800 years. The term *universitas*, after all, betokens a community recognized as able to look after its affairs. The early scholars did not just organize themselves and establish their own systems and orders ('standards' as we might term them these days), but were also formally recognized by the crown and the church as having the competence to do so. By and large, they were seen as having the right to control their own affairs and to go on developing their activities and communities as they saw fit. They were given similar freedom in the universities that they formed, and continued to have this until very recently.

Under these circumstances, a book with the title *Professional Development in Higher Education* could be taken to imply a number of things. It could indicate that, even though they have had several hundred years to get it right, academics have still not got around to taking their own development seriously. It could suggest that they have developed, but haven't worked out a serious account of what such self-development means. It could imply that the academics are having to see themselves in some sense as 'professionals' in a way that they have not had to do in the past. Perhaps academics pursued self-development without seeing themselves as professionals, but now that general perception has changed, they are choosing to develop their professionalism.

The story that Gill Nicholls offers is more concerned with the last of those possibilities; that it is time for academics to become explicit about their professionalism. At present, academics are being called to account by the rest of society and in the UK a new national body – the Institute for Learning and Teaching in Higher Education (ILT) – has been formed with the intention of encouraging and assisting the professionalization of academics.

Academics may say that they don't *need* to be professionalized; that the whole idea is an insult to their own professionalism that has been built up over hundreds of years. This point may well be true, but, as some of the possibilities listed earlier implied, academics could be discharging their own professionalism in even *better* ways. The new conditions faced by academics could make this task more challenging, so some collective thought – maybe under the aegis of their own professional body – could have some benefits.

Gill Nicholls argues that there are new conditions in academic life that are placing new challenges on the professionalism of academics and that their professionalism could be even better managed; indeed, she argues that the two issues are intertwined. Many of these new conditions are attached to professional life in general and to the character of modern society – they go well beyond academe *per se*. To use a fashionable term, society is now 'networked'. In the networked society there are few, if any, redoubts. Accordingly, professions can no longer enjoy complete control over their own affairs, as they are called to account by the many interests exerting legitimate claims on the character of the services offered. In the networked society, complexity reigns. It is increasingly difficult to predict the consequences that flow from any professional action or speech act.

The outcome of these developments, such as the call for greater transparency and the establishment of forms of personal and collective development, are well known. But as far as academics are concerned, there are three twists to the story which are articulated by Gill Nicholls.

Firstly, higher education has become so prized, its client base is now highly diverse and larger. In most professions, individuals engage with their clients on a one-to-one basis. In education, this exchange is often collective, with the professional engaging with many clients at a time. In higher education, this feature has been heightened by two developments: a change in the student:staff ratio which means that tutors are having to engage with extremely large numbers of students (often several hundred in a lecture theatre) and a sudden widening of the client group (terms such as 'inclusivity', 'diversity' and even 'rights' are beginning to replace 'participation' and 'access').

Secondly, academic life has allowed its activities to become skewed. 'Gladly wolde he lerne and gladly teche' were the twin characteristics of Chaucer's clerk – even in medieval times, there was an embryonic sense that teaching and research went hand in hand as the main *unifying* facets of academic life. For understandable reasons, an imbalance between these facets has developed across the Western world with the result that the greater part of academic life – its reward structure, values and self-understanding – is dedicated to research. It is clear that teaching still forms part of the balance, but is all too often seen as an adjunct of research enterprise or, worse still, is marginalized as research and teaching are pulled apart, fragmenting universities. As a result, insufficient attention is paid to learning and teaching. This forms an example of how academics' professionalism is being tested on a daily basis.

The third issue of academic professionalism involves the ideas of critical thought and increasing understanding. These ideas have been subjected to much buffeting of late from some philosophers and social theorists – the very idea that reflection can bring both autonomy and enlightenment, a notion embedded in Western philosophy, has been dented. However, in academe it lives on and, so long as such presuppositions are part of the conceptual foundations of universities, there is surely an obligation on academics to apply such presuppositions to their own practices, especially in relation to students' learning, the development of which universities are in business to promote.

Therefore, academics are finding that their professionalism is not just being tested; its very nature is having to be clarified and reformulated. There is no escape from this situation. The key issue is whether academics are going to take matters into their own hands and work out the character of their new professionalism by themselves or have it worked out for them, either by the haphazard exigencies of the unpredicted moment, or by a quasi-state body allowed to develop an orientation that is out of kilter with academics' own values, precisely because the academics declined to negotiate with it.

At present, it is possible for the academic community to realize itself as a *community* and to develop – as Gill Nicholls puts it – forms of 'reflexivity' that do justice to its interests in research and collective critique. These interests do not have to be separate from a widened sense of professionalism including teaching; indeed, they can help to realize that widened professionialism. It is just possible for the academic community to develop its *own* professionalism in these new times.

Ronald Barnett
Institute of Education, University of London

About the author

Gill Nicholls is Professor of Education in the School of Educational Studies at the University of Surrey where, among other responsibilities, she is Convenor of the Centre of Professional and Work Related Learning. Her research interests focus on professional development in education and on science education, and she has written and published widely on both subjects. Professor Nicholls' previous books include *Collaborative Change in Education* (1997) and *Learning to Teach* (1999) and she is Series Editor of the Kogan Page 'Teaching' series.

This book also includes a contribution from Jon Nixon, who has held chairs at Canterbury Christ Church University College and the University of Stirling. He is currently Professor of Educational Studies at the University of Sheffield. His recent writings have focused on the changing purposes and conditions of professional practice within the 'new' management of education. He is a founding Executive Editor of the academic journal *Teaching in Higher Education*.

1

The changing landscape

Introduction

> It was not a bad idea, whoever first conceived and proposed a public means
> for treating the sum of knowledge, in a quasi industrial manner, with a
> division of labour where, for so many fields as there may be of knowledge,
> so many public teachers would be allotted, professors being as trustees,
> forming together a kind of common scientific entity, called a university.
>
> (Immanuel Kant, 1798, 1979: 23)

Kant's perception in 1798 still has a poignancy and relevance today. His recognition
of the conflicts between knowledge creation and teaching, which surround academic
life, were insightful and definitive in his time and are arguably even more relevant to the changing landscape of higher education today. One of Kant's premises
related to the conflict surrounding what he termed 'thinkers in the university and
businessmen of knowledge', respectively creators and traders of knowledge. This
tension between producing knowledge and transmitting knowledge is now a major
discussion point in governments and universities across the world, and is an issue
that still has not been resolved, but is under continual scrutiny.

The tensions related to the teaching–research nexus have been revisited many
times in the evolution of higher education. The regularity of this revisiting and the
discussions associated with it have increased as knowledge, knowledge production
and transmission through a variety of means including technology have also
increased. Added to this is the speed with which the integration of academic,
industrial and government research into universities has occurred, which has further fuelled the debates surrounding research and teaching quality. A consequence
of this has been the division of labour related to teaching and research. Whether
this division has been forced or has happened through osmosis is not completely
clear. However, it has led to a growing trend for academic teachers and high-level

professional researchers within a faculty to identify themselves less as teachers and more as subject specialists and researchers. As a consequence of this type of integration, a perception has developed in universities that, in general, teaching and research are not mutually exclusive. However, and ironically, many feel that while research is found to be positively associated with teaching effectiveness, teaching loads are considered as having a negative impact on the capacity to undertake research. In Kant's description nothing has changed. Yet, in the context of the wider view of higher education it is necessary to contextualize the research–teaching nexus as it stands at present. This in itself requires a consideration of the changing world of higher education, albeit a brief one.

The changing world of higher education

The research–teaching nexus has been established as a well-founded area of discussion, but cannot be seen in isolation. While the perceived differences between researchers and teachers have been gaining pace within the academic community, the higher education system itself has been and is still going through a process of change, by moving towards mass education and more formalized external regulation (Westergraad, 1991; Elton, 1992). The expansion within the sector has highlighted shortcomings in the types of teaching and learning environment universities provide for their students and staff (Hattie and Marsh, 1996; Rowland, 1996). Nixon (1997) suggests that 'higher education now has a less homogeneous student population, which in turn has led to a diversification of course content and structure as a means of differentiated learning'. It has become clear that the educational settings that exist have not been able to cater for an increased diversity of students and the way in which these various students learn. Equally important is the speed with which new technologies are influencing possible teaching–learning environments. Clearly then the changing nature of student intake, curriculum and pedagogy is affecting the way in which academics have to function.

A further complication to the situation of teaching and research has been the change occurring in staffing structures in higher education. Kogan suggests: 'The cohesion afforded by traditional structures is likely to be eroded as status and other differentials increase, especially between staff with permanent appointments and those in temporary or part-time contracts' (Kogan, Moses and El-Khawas, 1994: 62–63). This differential is currently increasing, with top-level academics having to produce high-profile research, while the day-to-day work of teaching and research in universities is, as Ainley (1994) suggests, 'sustained by a growing army of insecurely employed contract staff who make up to a third of all academic employees' (p 32).

These changes have left academics in a dilemma: do they concentrate on keeping up with innovations in teaching and learning, do they try to adapt to a changing student population, do they keep up with their research or do they try to do all of these? Many academics in an attempt to resolve their own dilemma have looked to the higher education's reward structures and systems to gain insight and reassurance into which direction to go. The reward system reveals without a shadow of a doubt why so many academics place their research before teaching even if they feel passionately about their teaching. *Research is rewarded*; teaching is not! A consequence of this is that 'the occupation of university teacher no longer automatically offers autonomy and status' (Nixon, 1996: 7).

Alongside the reward systems favouring research, research itself has become more specialized with evidence to show how the research taking place in universities has little or no connection with teaching. Thus the balance between research and teaching has grown weaker. Within the changing landscape the teaching–research nexus has not lost any of its fervour or prominence; it has intensified.

The intensity has been caused by an increased demand for the need to improve the quality of teaching found in higher education institutions. The debate has taken on another dimension in the face of increased pressure for research excellence from such external assessment procedures as the Research Assessment Exercise (RAE). The dichotomy of research or teaching has yet again taken centre stage, a stage that now includes external regulation and imposed professional development as a means of raising teaching quality. With these issues in mind, now is an appropriate time to re-evaluate the role of professional development and what teaching, learning and scholarship in higher education mean. It is important to consider why and how we find ourselves in the present situation. What has made the landscape change?

Historical background to the ILT

This section discusses the historical background to the inception of the Institute of Learning and Teaching (ILT), and places the role of professional development in higher education within that context. Following the Dearing Report and the Government White Paper on Higher Education, the role of professional development has not only changed but has been given new dimensions and directions. These include the need for new lecturers to enrol on induction courses and programmes that are assessed in some form. Within this context there has been the introduction of continuing professional development plans that are closely linked to appraisal, promotion and professional standing. Much of the current debate focuses on the establishment of the ILT and the implications this will have on higher education institutions in the future.

The Dearing Report

What makes the present situation especially interesting is the impact of recent reviews and reports on higher education including the influential National Committee of Inquiry into Higher Education (NCIHE) chaired by Sir Ron Dearing, and commonly known as the Dearing Report (NCIHE, 1997). This made recommendations that were to have significant implications for the status of teaching and the notion of professional development in higher education. One of the main features of the report was the inception of the ILT, and the notion of imposed or enforced professional development. The ILT was born out of the Dearing Report, which recommended the immediate establishment of a professional institution for learning and teaching. The main recommendations in the report were set out as follows:

> *Recommendation 13*
> We recommend that institutions of higher education begin immediately to develop or seek access to programmes for teacher training of their staff, if they do not have them, and that all institutions seek national accreditation of such programmes from the Institute for Learning and Teaching in Higher Education.
>
> (para 8.61)

> *Recommendation 14*
> We recommend that the representative bodies, in consultation with the funding bodies, should immediately establish a professional Institute for Learning and Teaching in Higher Education. The functions of the institute would be to accredit programmes of training for higher education teachers, to commission research and development in teaching and learning practices, and to stimulate innovation.
>
> (para 8.61)

Other key recommendations in the Dearing Report included Recommendation 6, which covered the prospective role of the ILT in respect of students with disabilities; it recommended that 'the learning needs of students with disabilities be included in its research and programme of accreditation and advisory activities'.

Recommendation 13 by implication suggests some form of 'enforced' development programme for new members within the higher education community. This is not to say that some institutions were not already involved in good practice and providing new staff with extensive induction programmes. However, the statement in the Dearing Report clearly gives professional development a different dimension, by implying that it is now expected and indeed a prerequisite for probation to be completed. Recommendation 48 suggests: 'Over the medium term, it should become the normal requirement that all new, full-time academic staff with teaching responsibilities are required to achieve at least associate membership of the Institute for Learning and Teaching for successful completion of their probationary period.'

Within this new environment of expectation and quasi-enforcement the Report also proposed that the Institute of Learning and Teaching could recognize levels of expertise in teaching by conferring various categories of membership, that of associate member, member and fellow. This suggests that development is no longer a choice but a requirement, which is differentiated through demands and expectations.

The Government's approval for such an institution was made clear in its response to the Dearing recommendations. The response states:

> The Government sees the new Institute for Learning and Teaching in Higher Education to be established by the higher education sector as having a key role to play in enhancing the professional skills and status of teachers in higher education and in spreading good teaching more widely. The Government's long term aim is to see all teachers in higher education carry a professional qualification.
>
> (DfEE, 1998: 19–23)

The nature of the professional qualification is as yet unresolved, as the ILT is not at present in the position to operate a 'licence to practise', nor does the higher education community appear to want such a licence. The Dearing Report envisaged that the successful completion of an accredited programme or pathway would be a normal requirement for successful completion of probation. This links into the concept of a 'licence to practise' as operated by many professional bodies. The recommendations did not stop with initial entry, but suggested that continual professional development (CPD) be monitored and regulated. The report stated that:

> Membership of a professional body normally carries with it an obligation to remain in good standing, to maintain the level of one's professional expertise and to update one's knowledge on a regular basis. Thus, if it wishes to parallel the activities of other professional bodies, the Institute will need to establish:
> - Guidelines for regular commitment to CPD for all its categories of membership;
> - Procedures for verifying these activities in terms of demonstrable outcomes achieved.

These recommendations indicate the nature of the anticipated change that will be required, or even demanded, of the academic community. Within the context of this changing landscape of higher education, challenges are being made to some of the fundamental concepts and notions of what it is to be an academic. These challenges are proving contentious from a number of perspectives. At first sight it appears that the long-standing view of the autonomous academic is being threatened, as is the main perceived focus of academics' work, that of research. The notion of achieving a level of competence that matches a licence to practise is not only daunting to those primarily concerned with research, but is also conceived as an imposition to the academics' *raison d'être*. Such initial reaction led the consultation documents following Dearing to ask questions related to professional development and a licence to practise, among many other issues. The higher education community was asked to consider the following questions: 1) What kind of relationship, if any, should there be between the accreditation of programmes/pathways and any conferment of a licence to practise upon individual staff? 2) Should accreditation eventually become mandatory for all teaching staff?

Institutional responses to these questions varied considerably. In the context of the changing landscape it is important to consider the implications of introducing imposed professional development to meet criteria of a professional body. The criteria as suggested by the ILT raise issues about academics as professionals, and their anticipated behaviour as professionals within a professional body. These issues are dealt with extensively in Chapters 2 and 5. However, it is necessary to highlight here the way these changes are taking place. Suggesting that the academic community requires a professional body assumes that academics do not already engage with this level of professionalism. It also assumes that throughout the academic community there is more bad practice than good in the areas of teaching and learning, and hence that teaching and learning support needs monitoring in a formalized way, requiring competence to be shown, accredited and rewarded by membership to the professional body. It is these assumptions that are questioned and discussed in this book.

Establishing the Institute for Learning and Teaching

The remit for implementing the recommendations of the Dearing Report were given to the Institute for Learning and Teaching Planning Group (ILTPG), led by Professor Roger King and comprising representatives of a range of key stakeholder organizations within higher education. (Terms of reference can be found as Appendix A of the Dearing Report.)

The planning group's remit was to shape the creation and establishment of the ILT. This was to be established by taking account of views within both the higher education sector and other professional bodies associated with higher education. These included the UK funding bodies, higher education teaching unions and the Quality Assurance Agency (QAA). Through a consultative forum and six working groups the ILTPG attempted to sketch and develop a working framework for the ILT. A main aim for this framework was given at the launch of the ILTPG, when Professor King stated: 'Higher education students require high quality teaching. The new institute will build on good practice, which has been developed in recent years, and seek its widest promotion and dissemination. This will help ensure that the role of teaching in universities and colleges gets the attention and status it deserves' (this can be accessed by visiting www.hefce.ac.uk).

Following the first round of consultation a report was published in October 1997. This showed good practice existed in the preparation of staff for teaching and learning roles. The Teaching Quality Assessment reports of the Higher Education Funding Council (HEFC) and the Learning from Audit reports of the Higher Education Quality Council (HEQC) subsequently confirmed this. The reports also pointed to considerable deficiencies, suggesting that there had been significant growth over recent years in staff development for teaching roles, and that induction programmes for teaching staff were technically mandatory in over half of all English universities. However, by no means all eligible staff were enabled to take part in practice.

Interestingly the October report concluded that existing opportunities, participation levels and schemes of monitoring and evaluation for professional development in teaching and learning were unevenly distributed. Their recommendations to these findings were that a system of accreditation was needed that encouraged good practice, raised the quality of provision across the whole of higher education and conferred recognition on the professionalism of staff not only for their teaching and learning roles but also in 'academic practice'. The report defined 'academic practice' as covering the full range of professional activities undertaken by academics – including research and administration as well as teaching and learning.

The report also suggested the following:

- that initial professional development should be seen as part of, and not separate from, continual professional development;
- recognizing the importance of subject-specific teaching contexts;
- the value of teaching observation;
- the desirability of extending continuing professional development;
- staff having access to routes of professional recognition.

All the suggestions and recommendations were in keeping with the Dearing Report, which made clear that the ILT was to provide 'professional standing' for teachers in higher education. This perception is a difficult one for the higher education community to accept, as stated earlier, because although teaching and research have the rhetoric of equal importance in differing contexts, in reality research has the greater status. After all, research as a *raison d'être* of academic life has been confirmed by the various RAEs (1992, 1996, 2001). The Dearing Report itself stated that 'one current barrier is that staff perceive national and international policies as actively encouraging and recognizing excellence in research, but not teaching' (p 32).

Against this background the ILTPG recommended that a key function of the ILT would be to attempt to 'redress the balance between teaching and research' by providing a national focus for teaching. It is an accepted principle that a key function of the ILT is to 'improve the quality of teaching and learning in higher education', but how and on what evidence? These are interesting questions, as the notion of improvement suggests that there is at present a deficit or a perceived deficit of quality. Yet, 'there is little national evidence to suggest that the standards in teaching in higher education require systematic improvement' (DfEE, 1999: 3). It is, however, accepted that the challenges and landscape of teaching in higher education are becoming greater and more diverse, with a rapid growth of knowledge, a growing, diverse student population and a culture for lifelong learning.

The above challenges to the sector require the maintenance of teaching quality and the development of new and innovative methods of teaching. If the ILT is to impact on the higher education community's views of teaching, it must have a clear purpose and set areas of provision. The ILT's purpose and functions are discussed in detail in Chapter 2, but the key functions can be summarized as follows:

- accreditation;
- development and dissemination;
- membership services.

The areas of provision can be summarized as follows:

- to enhance the status of teaching in higher education;
- to maintain and improve the quality of learning and teaching in higher education;
- to set standards of good professional practice that its members, and in due course all those with learning and teaching responsibilities, might follow.

The Dearing Report envisaged that the ILT should be a professional body for teachers and related staff in higher education. All the consultation feedback showed widespread agreement that the ILT should be a practitioner organization, the preferred model being that of a professional body that operates as a learned society with self-regulated membership levels. The Government's response to the Dearing Report, *Higher Education for the 21st Century*, is indicative of the types of development that will be required by higher education communities in the future. Chapter 3 of the Government's response is directed at learning and teaching and starts with the statement: 'A better balance is needed in higher education between teaching, research and scholarship. The Government aims to encourage strategies that promote effective learning and teaching and enhance the professional skills and status of teachers' (DfEE, 1998: 19).

To ensure such initiatives are implemented, the Government in conjunction with the HEFC have 'encouraged institutions to give high priority to developing and implementing learning and teaching strategies which focus on the promotion of students' learning' (p 19). To give substance to this statement the Government has given clear indication that it will monitor progress made by institutions in the area of teaching and learning as a means of assuring the quality of teaching, and the maintenance and raising of standards, as well as the way in which institutions respond to national policy. Further reinforcement of the Government's pledge to improve standards was given in a statement indicating that a review of progress made and further steps required would occur within a five-year period.

What are the implications of such requirements and the perceived nature of the development courses that members of the higher education community with responsibilities for teaching are likely to incur? With Government set on improving the quality of teaching and the universities' need to maintain research excellence, it would seem that compromise is needed. But one must ask the question: compromise what and how? Research shows that institutions provide their staff with courses that are mandatory but that the release of staff for such courses is not always what it should be. Yet the Government has specified that it is its long-term aim to see all teachers in higher education carry a professional qualification, achieved by meeting demanding standards of teaching and supervisory competence through accredited training or experience (DfEE, 1998: 43).

The idea of professional development

Professional development is a phrase that continually appears in the literature related to the ILT and teaching quality. But how will this have a bearing on future needs and direction within the higher education community? Chapter 3 looks at these issues in detail, but here it is sufficient to raise some of the issues that should be taken into consideration when trying to influence and shape the future landscape.

The concept and provision for professional development is, by its very nature, highly complex and multifaceted. Inherent in many of the arguments related to professional development and the learning society is the belief that change is constant and inevitable (Baptiste, 1999; Watson and Taylor, 1998; Edwards, 1997). Change and particularly the unpredictability of change is often held to be a central characteristic of the contemporary world. Often changes external to the world of education and training are developed to act as a rationale for change within that world (Edwards, 1997).

The main focus of the argument is that professional development is one aspect of learning and a way in which practitioners can understand the need to change, and that this involves continual learning, whether formally or informally. As Jarvis (1999) states, 'there are profound implications for their [the practitioners] continuing learning, since they are learning incidentally and informally in practice all the time'. He goes on to say: 'Formal continuing learning programmes need to be relevant to what they actually do and must contain opportunities for testing ideas and theories' (p 169). Bearing these comments in mind the main focus for the discussion here will be the new teacher in British universities. It will concentrate on the type of learning that Jarvis considers to be 'more formal, guided and the type of learning that occurs when practitioners and practitioner-researchers undertake a programme of continuing professional education' (p 169).

This more formal learning is referred to as professional development, which is reflected in induction programmes of teaching and learning as required by the ILT. Crucial to the debate of formalized learning is an understanding of the context in which such formalization is occurring in universities at present. That context is the changing landscape of higher education, and specifically refers to enhancing the quality of teaching and learning through formalized and imposed induction professional development courses.

Meeting the challenges of the changing landscape

Meeting the challenges of the changing landscape will require academics to reflect on what their future roles may entail, and how they perceive the mechanisms by which they will meet the challenges of that changing role. Many institutions have been offering courses in teaching and learning for many years. Independent associations such as the Staff Educational Development Association (SEDA) and the University Co-ordination, Staff Development Association (UCoSDA) have also provided opportunities and pathways for academics to gain certification and accreditation for teaching in higher education. But, despite this the landscape has changed. Professional development related to teaching and learning has now become imposed. All new academics have to adhere to this imposition, and in the future all experienced academics will have to meet some form of imposed requirements. Competence in the field of teaching and learning will not only be expected but will have to be demonstrated.

New entrants to the academy will need to complete courses that allow them to demonstrate their competence in the areas of teaching and learning. These areas will be assessed in a variety of ways, including peer observation and project work. Experienced academics will have a direct entry route to the ILT for a limited period. What the nature and criteria for membership will be after this time is still not clear. But something will be required. These demands in themselves show the challenges academics have to face.

Meeting the challenges of the changing landscape also requires the academic community to engage more with research and findings related to teaching and learning. Dearing made this clear in his recommendations. Let us consider what is expected by considering statements from Dearing:

> [Placing] higher education on a more professional basis requires a strong foundation of theoretical and practical research into the learning and teaching process [8.64]... It is especially important that research outcomes are well used to inform policy and improve practice (and stimulate innovation) in learning and teaching [8.68]... There is no place, at present, where such a body of knowledge can be developed... [And] there is no agency to fund, commission or co-ordinate such research [8.64].

The committee went on to point out:

> We find it surprising that there has been little strategic research to monitor the consequences of recent changes in the students' learning environments and institutions' teaching activities. Although there is a substantial body of research about student learning, there has been little follow-up work into how some accepted principles might be translated into new teaching practices across disciplines and professional areas [8.19].

This failure of the higher education system to monitor the changes recently introduced to higher education or to take adequate notice of existing research findings has been recgonised . Entwistle (1998) commented at the SRHE/CVCP seminar: as 'teaching in higher education relies substantially on the critical analysis of research-based evidence, the lack of attention to research on learning and teaching was seen as somewhat paradoxical'.

Thinking of research on student learning as a means of creating a more effective learning community is not new. However, Entwistle suggests (p 2):

The ILT should encourage useful research into learning and teaching by ensuring a more direct focus for research on current developments in higher education. Conceptual research has tended not to be policy orientated, while the development work has been somewhat atheoretical and often inadequate in methodological terms. The ILT should bring together conceptual research with development work, and disseminate the findings in an accessible form so as to encourage high quality learning and a more cost-effective use of teaching resources.

Entwistle's suggestion poses a challenge not only to the ILT but the academic community too. If evidence is to be disseminated in a way that academics can engage in, which must be considered as a good step forward, then the next step is ensuring that academics engage with the evidence and can reflect on that engagement in such a way as to improve practice. Chapter 6 examines some of these issues, and pays particular attention to teaching, research and scholarship, and the possible relationships they may have. It challenges the notions of research into teaching and learning and suggests ways in which academics may wish to review what it is to be engaged in teaching, research and scholarship. As Boyer (1990) stated, the scholarship of teaching is distinct from the scholarship of discovery – but it is still scholarship and not just teaching. As there is no (statistical) relationship between excellence in research and excellence in teaching at the level of the individual scholar (Terenzini and Pascarella, 1994), improving teaching must involve more than improving research. It has to involve improving the scholarship of teaching and this involves lecturers using literature and contributing to the literature (Gibbs, 1998). This is a dimension of professional development that must be seen as a fundamental feature of future developmental programmes if the status and effectiveness of good teaching in higher education are to be secured.

There is no doubt that if academics in higher education are to be encouraged to engage with research into learning and teaching and to contribute to any future work in the field they will have to perceive the exercise as worth while. Chapter 4 considers the moves towards making academics engage in research and reflection within the field of learning and teaching. It challenges the notion of assessing the products of reflection and engagement with the literature surrounding educational research, on the grounds that academics will write reports to meet criteria rather than truly connect with research and reflection in the field of teaching and learning. It argues that the accreditation process should require teachers to demonstrate that they can use pedagogic literature to analyse and develop their teaching, rather than concentrate on the outcomes of their changed pedagogic practice.

What are we faced with? An academic community that has to face change and a type of change that challenges many of the underlying beliefs surrounding the role of the academic. To meet these challenges head-on requires an element of risk for the individual. The notion of risk and the consequences it may have for the individual are discussed in Chapter 6. Risk may be considered from a variety of perspectives, concerning the implication of actions by the individual and the institution. Teaching and research do not happen in a vacuum, and each has repercussions on the individual at both personal and institutional level. Continual challenges of change within a community that has undergone and is still undergoing speedy and significant change can and do impinge on the personal development of the individual, and this impingement reflects on the performance of the institution. Managing these changes and challenges, both personally and institutionally, is a theme throughout this book. Maybe the time has come to ask the question: what lies beyond the ILT? This forms the content of the last chapter, where I suggest ways forward for future thinking related to teacher accreditation in higher education, and the ways in which academics may wish to show their development in the areas of learning and teaching.

2

The demands and functions of the ILT

Introduction

This chapter will consider the demands and proposed functions of the Institute for Learning and Teaching. It will contextualize these in terms of what it is to engage in a competency-based system of development and how this in turn may affect the nature, purpose and engagement of academics in their training as teachers, as well as in their activities related to professional development. Although a contemporary context is given, the issues that are put forward are taken beyond the immediate and used as a means of questioning the reasons and rationale for some of the demands made by the ILT and the long-term implications these demands may have on the future development of members of the academic community. Professional development programmes based on a competency approach are discussed in terms of their relevance to the academic community, especially as that community is at present generally research-led and not teaching-led. The discussion is placed within the context of the ILT being a professional body, established for professionals engaged in teaching and the support of learning.

Establishing a perceived need for the ILT

University teaching might be called the hidden profession. It is practised as a secret rite behind closed doors and is not mentioned in polite academic society.

(Mathews, 1963)

Prior to the Dearing Report (NCIHE, 1997), it might have been possible to support this view of teaching in many British universities. It was a view that assumed teaching skills to be conferred on lecturers as a postgraduate gift, one that it was neither appropriate nor necessary to inquire into or closely scrutinize. Communication of knowledge was considered secondary to its advancement, the balance between teaching and research being heavily biased towards the latter. During the 60s Mathews (1963) was quoted as saying, 'In no other aspect of their work were academics apparently lacking in critical inquiry'. The major thrust of his text was to demonstrate that at that point in time there appeared to be no literature to indicate that there were detectable problems in teaching and learning in higher education, nor did teaching in higher education appear to be a problem worthy of attention.

Three important reports emerged during the 60s, namely the Hale Report (1964), the Brynmor Jones Report (1965) and the Parry Report (1967), all examining general aspects of teaching and learning in universities. Research units were set up to establish and investigate the problems of higher education and inquiries into teaching methods. At this juncture it is interesting to consider a statement from Layton (1968) regarding the issue and problems surrounding teaching and learning in higher education:

> In so far as teaching can be described as an activity in which a teacher, aided by various materials, resources, initiates students into mastery of selected knowledge, skills and attitudes, it is true to say that all four elements of the activity – teachers, communication, resources, students and body of knowledge – are currently undergoing change. The democratisation of higher education has produced the confrontation of 'new student' and 'new teacher'; the rapid expansion of knowledge has posed unprecedented teaching problems.

Layton goes on to say: 'On this turbulent picture must be overlaid the consideration that the economic significance of higher education has been firmly grasped and that, in Sir Eric Asby's phrase, higher education has become a critical industry' (p viii).

These statements should make one stop and ask: why has nothing changed 32 years later? Why are we rehearsing the same arguments? Why do we still have a teaching–research nexus? Why is teaching still causing consternation in higher education? Will the ILT make a difference to this perpetual nexus or will it compound the difficulties already present within higher education? Are the demands and expectations of the ILT realistic and feasible?

These questions are key in the future development of the learning environments of higher education, especially when put in the context of the Dearing

Report and the implications that it holds for the future of teaching and learning, and the consequent professional development of academics. Dearing stated uncompromisingly: 'Institutions and their staff face a great challenge if our vision that the United Kingdom should be at the forefront of world practice in learning and teaching in higher education is to be realised' (paragraph 8.56).

This suggests that attention needs to be focused on university teaching, but interestingly one must ask the question whether the focus on teaching is just one aspect of concern within a larger and more complex problem. What is at stake is the ability of universities to adapt to the economic and social demands of society, whilst at the same time remaining centres of intellectual excellence, discovery and innovation. Here again Dearing makes reference to these issues and suggests that academics within universities must keep up to date through continual professional development. He suggests that 'forms of professional development should not be restricted to those at the beginning of their careers, or to those groups with a formal responsibility for teaching'. This implies that career-long development through systematic updating in the discipline and in the pedagogy can equip academics who are involved in and support learning, of both students and other academics. How different is this from 30 years ago?

The language of Dearing may be different, but in essence the contention is the same. In order for universities to respond to changing work environments, technological innovations and social conditions, as well as remaining competitive at international, national and regional level, there needs to be a major commitment to continue systematic upgrading, extending, developing and retaining of teaching/learning skills by institutions of higher education.

This does not imply that what is now required in higher education is a detailed inventory of techniques and problems over a broad front of teaching/learning skills; what is urgently needed is inquiries into the effectiveness of particular methods and practices associated with specific courses and disciplines. This type of inquiry is essential if in the long term our knowledge of teaching/learning methods and environments is to be based on more than opinion and anecdotal evidence. These inquiries are also needed to ensure that future professional development programmes are at the cutting edge of effective practice.

The thrust of the argument is that higher education should be looking to what is effective practice and how best this can be disseminated and engaged in. The Government's view of this is based on the Dearing Report; it was, and still is, the achievement of these aims through the establishment of the ILT. Chapter 1 has traced and illustrated the 'birth' and subsequent development of the ILT. It has also suggested that all is not necessarily well in the garden of professional development. I introduced this chapter by suggesting that the notion of 'all not being well' in the teaching/learning and professional development of those in higher education is a well-diagnosed and established 'illness'. What has not been tackled is how the perceived illness may or may not be cured or at the very least managed. Continuing the medical analogy, one can assume that the ILT has been constructed, in the first instance, to establish mechanisms by which the 'illness' can be tracked, monitored, managed and, it is hoped, eventually cured, or even that the ILT has been constructed to prevent the illness. Or will it be forced to palliative care?

This then raises the question: what are the demands of the ILT and how are these perceived as managing, enhancing, creating and developing new frameworks and structures in order to prevent deterioration of the 'illness' (in this case perceived bad teaching, learning and CPD opportunities of those in higher education)?

Before an exploration and critique are made of the ILT demands, it is important to contextualize the nature and provision of training and development of lecturers in higher education. It would be foolish to say that as a community higher education has not looked at and tried to improve teaching and learning over the last 32 years. Despite the same questions being raised by those in government office, organizations such as SEDA and UCoSDA have through a variety of means engaged many academics in the development of teaching and learning skills over the years.

SEDA began the development of an accreditation scheme for teachers in higher education in 1990 and launched the teacher accreditation scheme in 1992. Since then 61 programmes to train university teachers have been recognized, and a further 15 are being prepared for recognition, with over 1000 teachers being accredited by SEDA. Similar initiatives can be found for UCoSDA. These figures, although small, suggest that movement to recognize teaching and learning in higher education has been gathering momentum within the higher education community, albeit slowly. What is it then that the ILT proposes that will ensure a speedy and effective training of higher education teachers? Equally important is to ask: is this the correct strategy and where might we be in 5 or 10 years' time?

Demands of the ILT

These have changed and continue to change as this book is being written. For this reason it is necessary to explore what the demands were, how they have changed, what they are now and what they may be in the future. The demands will have, and already have had, implications on those involved in teaching and learning in the higher education community.

Early requirements and recommendations

The proposed functions of the ILT following the Dearing Report had three main purposes:

1. the accreditation of programmes of training for higher education teachers;
2. the research and development in teaching and learning;
3. the stimulation of innovation.

The implications of each of these elements needs clarification and contextualizing, if we are to understand how and why the ILT has positioned itself within the higher education community, and as a result how it might influence future professional development activities, innovations and demands.

The introduction of accredited programmes is an interesting one, bearing in mind that SEDA and UCoSDA already provided such possibilities for academics. However, what is being conceived now through the ILT is a national accreditation system for higher education, of which participation is not in essence through choice. The national accreditation group chaired by Booth sent out consultation documents relating to a national accreditation system, receiving a 77 per cent support response to an accreditation scheme. The Booth Report suggested 'an approach to accreditation whereby institutions would be required to map their provision onto a national statement of broad outcomes, underpinning knowledge and core professional and ethical values' (Accreditation and Teaching in Higher Education Planning Group, 1998: 6).

This proposed approach was intended to provide a framework around which individual institutions (or consortia) could plan and develop their own pathways and programmes. While the Booth Report set out a broad framework for the development of a national accreditation scheme, the proposed ILT was to be responsible for other areas, including a licence to practise, continuing professional development and levels of membership.

The Dearing Report made clear links between accreditation and the concept of a 'licence to practise'. This has raised and continues to raise significant questions relating to the mandatory nature of such a concept, in terms of relationships between accreditation of pathways and the conferment of any such licence. Associated with this concept of 'licence to teach' is the maintenance of such a licence through continual professional development (CPD). As with any professional body it was assumed that there would be an obligation to carry out CPD as a means of maintaining professional knowledge, the implication also being that any CPD activity would have to be verified in terms of demonstrable outcomes achieved. The Booth Report recommended 5–8 days per annum for CPD activities.

The whole nature of these early recommendations assumed, and continues to assume, certain precepts regarding academics' engagement in CPD, the basic precept being that academics are not already professionals and thus engaged in professional development in a systematic way. The consequence of this precept is that a large infrastructure such as the ILT is required to make academics professional. One needs to ask on what evidence these early assumptions related to CPD were based.

Academics' professionalism emerges, as in the past, from their subject-based societies or organizations, which take (and took) an active interest in teaching and learning environments. It is not surprising then that many questions and challenges were brought to the demands laid by the ILT regarding CPD, levels of membership and what such a 'professional body' might actually give academics that they do not already have access to.

Levels of membership

Within the national framework the proposed structure was to have three levels of membership, those of associate member, member and fellow. The Booth Report focused primarily on associate member status; however, it also sketched out some indicative criteria for higher levels of membership (see Table 2.1). The criteria focused on mainstream teaching and learning activities, which were to be broadened to include activities carried out by other staff in support of teaching and learning. It is worth pausing here to consider some of the responses in relation to accreditation issues.

Most responses embraced the view that the accreditation of teachers in higher education would be a powerful force for raising standards of teaching and learning. However, not all elements were embraced equally. SEDA's response was quite clear:

> The current document is disappointing. It represents in several aspects a step backward from the widely accepted recommendations of the Booth Committee last year. Specifically, the proposed outcomes are over-prescriptive, unhelpful and unclear. They appear unnecessarily daunting to both new and experienced teachers, as well as those who develop and run courses to train teachers... The CPD proposals look over complex, although the principle of accredited CPD is strongly welcomed. Overall what is needed is a clear framework of outcomes, underpinning professional philosophy and underpinning knowledge and processes.
>
> (SEDA, 1998)

Table 2.1   Booth's committee membership framework

Category or Level of Membership	Illustrative Range of Responsibility
Associate Part 1	Classroom practice, marking, evaluation of teaching.
Associate Part 2	In addition to above: Design of a module, unit or series of teaching sessions, design of assessment, evaluation of modules.
Member	In addition to the above: Curriculum/programme design (eg across a degree), improvement of curricula/programmes, innovation in own course practice, evaluation of programmes, supervision of associates.
Fellow	In addition to the above: Leader of change (across institutions or disciplines) in teaching or curricula, through research, publications, work on disciplinary or professional bodies.

The second aspect of the initial consultation focused on research and development. Here the Dearing Report looked to the ILT commissioning analyses of various educational organizational practices and developments. The ILT could also have a role in researching the impact of national policies on teaching and learning effectiveness, a key element being that of sharing and disseminating a knowledge base related to teaching and learning. The third function was to use research outcomes to stimulate innovation, including possible kitemarking of computer-based learning materials (Recommendation 15).

These views, as with all aspects of the ILT's proposed infrastructure, went to consultation, which was followed by further documents titled *The Institute for Learning and Teaching: Implementing the vision* and *The National Framework for Higher Education* (NCIHE, 1997). These documents formalized the inception of the ILT, its terms of reference and the nature of the framework to be imposed, as well as criteria and routes for membership.

The national framework for higher education teaching has clear specifications and demands. These are summarized as follows:

> We have specified the requirements for ILT membership in terms of a range of teaching outcomes, by which we mean the knowledge, under-standing and range of skills and values that a teacher acquires through training and/or experience. We believe that there should be two categories of membership – Member and Associate member, distinguished by the range of outcomes achieved by candidates and their level of professional autonomy and responsibility.
>
> We have identified five broad areas of responsibility associated with HE teaching and suggest that members should be expected to achieve all or most of the outcomes linked under these headings, and that associate members should be expected to achieve about half.

It was assumed that experienced staff were likely to possess most if not all of the evidence they would need to demonstrate the stated outcomes. On the other hand it was assumed that inexperienced staff would, over a period of time, assemble evidence whilst following an accredited programme or pathway of staff development that would help them meet the needs and demands of ILT membership.

The implication of the proposed framework can be considered from two perspectives. The first relates to the immediate, what it means to be a member of the ILT and the alternative routes to membership. The second relates to the wider context of the demands being set and required of academics, both experienced and inexperienced. The wider context takes account of notions of professionalism, autonomy, self-development and the academic community as a whole.

Routes to membership

The ILT, having been set up as a professional body for higher education staff involved in teaching and the support of learning, is envisaged in time as being the main source of professional recognition for those engaged in teaching and learning support in higher education. Members of this professional institution would be able to:

- obtain recognition for the professionalism of their teaching;
- keep updated on developments in teaching and learning in HE and on methods of self-evaluation and improvement;
- obtain information and guidance on implementing new learning and teaching strategies, including ICT;
- have access to new research, publications and conference seminars.

The proposed routes to membership and the criteria by which routes are identified have key features that are based on five areas of professional activity:

1. teaching and/or supporting learning in HE;
2. contribution to the design and planning of learning activities and/or programmes of study;
3. provision of feedback and assessment of students' learning;
4. contribution to the development of effective learning environments and student support systems;
5. reflection on personal practice in teaching and learning and work on improving the teaching process.

Within these five professional areas it is also stated that:

● Initial membership routes would be designed to recognize and reflect the current expertise of experienced staff.
● There would be both individual and institutionally based routes that reflect the diversity of educational contexts within the sector. Individuals would be able to apply for membership directly to the ILT, rather than through an institution, if they wished.
● The membership criteria would be informed by underpinning knowledge and professional values including commitments to learning and scholarship as an integral part of teaching.

Continual professional development

The national framework sets out clear criteria and expectations for the nature and quantity of the continual professional development (CPD) required by academics. The document sets out a considerable amount of prescription within what constitutes CPD, as well as the outcomes expected from engagement in CPD activities. The terminology used is forceful and directive, introducing terms such as professional competence, conformity, outcomes, required documents and obligation. How can this be interpreted within a community as diverse as higher education, where many if not most academics are involved in CPD through their discipline-based societies or learned bodies? What does it mean for an experienced academic to 'remain in good standing'?

From an ILT perspective this requires academics to keep a personal professional development record (PDR) to support teaching. The principles underpinning this development record are that:

- systematic updating and planned improvement of professional competence throughout individual members' working lives are necessary to support career progression and to respond to changing work environments;
- whilst ILT members are responsible for deciding on the precise means by which they meet the requirements to remain in good standing, the character of CPD activities may be influenced by institutional policies and practices;
- members have a professional obligation to maintain currency in both their specialist subject area(s) and in the pedagogy of that subject, and to demonstrate this commitment ILT members should present their evidence in an accessible format that allows for easy scrutiny;
- the ILT has a duty to assure itself, the public and other bodies that its members adhere to the requirements of the national framework in terms of their professional competence and conduct, and that it will establish mechanisms for the periodic verification of its members' professional development records;
- the ILT has a responsibility to provide best practice guidance on CPD to its members and to support their professional development.

Following these underlying principles the framework elaborates the need for appropriateness of CPD activities, and that these 'collectively' will enable members to demonstrate convincingly that they 'remain in good standing' in their profession. Evidence is to be drawn from:

- professional work-based activities;
- personal activities outside work;
- courses, seminars, conferences and training events;
- self-directed and informal learning.

An average time of 40 hours per year would be required by the ILT to satisfy CPD guidelines.

The stated demands are clear and specific in the sense that they are prescriptive and appear to be definitive in their requirements. Yet there is ambiguity about what might constitute evidence and the proportion of personal and professional documentation required within a portfolio of CPD. It is interesting here to consider the nature of the responses gained from professional bodies already assisting academic staff with their development. SEDA, discussing the proposed framework, stated that:

> The current document is disappointing. It represents in several aspects a step backward from the widely accepted recommendations of the Booth Committee... Specifically, the proposed outcomes are over-prescriptive, unhelpful and unclear. They appear unnecessarily daunting to both new

and experienced teachers, as well as to those who develop and run courses to train teachers. The view is seductive losing the integrated view of teaching provided by Booth. The underpinning professional values and knowledge, which were a strong feature of Booth, have been substantially lost, replaced by an NV-like form of expression that is much less acceptable to the sector. The CPD proposals look over complex, although the principle of accredited CPD is strongly welcomed.

(SEDA, 1998)

What is problematic with the proposed CPD is that the guidelines are inappropriately over-specific as to the forms of evidence required. A possible interpretation is that those CPD requirements should allow individuals to develop both breadth and depth in the work they do as teachers. It is also important that members' standing be maintained in respect of their pedagogy within their subject, a view reiterated by all in higher education. So why is it that we need such prescription? The ILT's proposed national framework was hoping to establish a professional body for academics related to learning and teaching, thus raising the profile, status and standards of teaching within the higher education community. In order to understand why one might think a professional body such as the ILT might be required and why the ILT thinks it should be a professional body for the learning and teaching of academics in higher education, it is necessary to explore the issues. Consideration of what constitutes a professional body, the requirements for classification as a professional and the criteria for gaining professional standing with respect to other professions will allow me to contextualize why the ILT believes it can demand and expect certain levels of competence and standards from its membership.

Implications for a 'professional' within higher education

In Chapter 5, Jon Nixon considers the notion of a 'new professionalism' for the academic and how in a utopian way this may be conceived. Why this debate is needed will become clear as consideration is given to how the ILT would, could or should change the nature of the professional academic if its prescriptive approach remains.

First, what is a profession? A profession is a particular sort of full-time occupation, the practice of which presupposes a specialized educational background. Specialized education allows the professional to secure practical and theoretical expertise relevant to his or her field as well as to acquire general knowledge and a sense of ethical values (Siegrist, 1994: 4). Knowledge that is utilized 'selflessly' for the common welfare regardless of person is guaranteed through examination and licence (p 4). This being the case, professions demand, therefore, exclusive control over certain areas of operation and service as well as freedom from external supervision. In addition, a well-organized profession possesses autonomous control over admissions and licensing policies, which are closely mapped to competence, ethics and values associated with the profession. Based on this premise members of a professional body can lay claim to 'higher status'. In order to gain this status a process of 'professionalization' takes place.

What are the implications of the above statements and definitions to the demands of the ILT? The Dearing Report clearly stated that the ILT be set up as the 'professional body' for higher education staff involved in teaching and the support of learning. As such this is the mission of the ILT. Incumbent in its aims is that it will be 'governed by its members', 'reflect their professional values' and be the source of professional recognition. A first consideration of these claims suggests that the demands requested by the ILT appear in congruence with the demands and perceptions of a professional body and a professional. It would also appear to be acceptable to demand a certain level of competence to be gained through the professionalization process as prescribed by the ILT, as it claims to be the 'professional body' for higher education teachers.

This is all well and good, but there is one crucial element missing in this discussion of professional body, professions and professionalization in respect of the ILT, and that is a political dimension. The ILT is a 'professional body' conceived by the Dearing Report and implemented by political intervention. 'Professionals' within the higher education sector did not demand the ILT, as most academics already belonged to a professional body related to their discipline area. As such the conception of the ILT was, and remains, an imposition on the higher education community, one that requires all new members to join and strongly encourages experienced members to do so. The question that needs to be asked is: will the nature of the imposition and the types of demands required by the ILT ensure a professional body with the calibre of professionals within it that the ILT suggests it will procure?

To assume all academics will join the ILT irrespective of their 'competence', by making membership a declared necessity, is to ignore the dynamic relationship between academics and their environment, as well as the nature of the 'professional' the ILT is attempting to create.

The ILT's positioning on these issues says a great deal about its possible relationship with state, government and the 'profession' it suggests it is supporting. Can it be that the state determines the structures and market of higher education and through its policies ensures that, in certain cases, only the certification of warranted professionals is recognized? If all institutions have to meet the demands of the ILT by being accredited to them for their teaching and learning courses, this ensures in principle that all new entrants to the 'profession' of learning and teaching are members of the 'professionals' body'. At the same time a fast-track option is provided for experienced staff as a means of encouragement to join the professional body. This fast track to membership will only be available for the first three years, from the inception of the ILT, thus ensuring a critical mass of members.

When this is achieved will the ILT, reinforced by state approval and control, through issues such as widening participation, start to control entry to and practice of the profession, for example 'no membership, no opportunity' in the higher education community, or a regulated salary structure based on 'professional standing and competence'? Examples of the pressure higher education institutions feel under to comply with membership is shown in the increasing number of advertisements for posts requiring applicants to demonstrate that they are able to provide evidence for entry to the ILT as part of the application procedures. These are serious and complex issues, but ones that should not be ignored; as Becher (1994: 1–2) suggests, the means by which governments, whether national, regional or local, set out to control the activities of the professions are many and diverse, as are the motives for seeking control.

Seeking control through competence and standards

If the ILT, through state persuasion, is looking for a more competent and effective community of higher education teachers, then the notion of competence must be looked at in terms of the relevance it has to the actual task at hand, that of making academics better or more effective teachers in the higher education community. If control is to be sought or imposed it is important to consider the role of competence within a 'professional setting'. As stated earlier, the ILT requires evidence of competence. The discourse related to competence is not new, and has been well rehearsed in the area of initial teacher training, as well as within the higher education sector. Barnett in his book *The Limits of Competence* puts forward the argument (1994: 159):

> Competence is an entirely acceptable aim for the academic community. We want our doctors, accountants and even philosophers to be competent. We may want more than competence from them but, still, competence remains a near-universal virtue. Competence, then, is not problematic in itself as an educational aim, even in higher education. If competence is an acceptable aim, then it is essential that the nature and context are well articulated so that those who have to demonstrate competence are clear of its aims. Competence becomes problematic when it becomes the dominant aim, so diminishing other worthwhile aims; or when competence is constructed over-narrowly.

Clearly from the above argument we would expect competence from our academics in the areas of teaching and learning. However, if they are to demonstrate such competence and be accepted as professionals within the professional body, they must have a clear and well-constructed framework in which to develop and demonstrate their competence in an appropriate way. At present the requirements to demonstrate competence are neither clear nor well constructed, leaving academics wishing to engage with CPD in a meaningful way at the very least confused or in the extreme sceptical and non-compliant.

Barnett's (1994: 160) interpretation of 'operational' and 'academic' competence is useful here as it helps to highlight the confusion caused by the demand of the CPD requirements as laid down in the ILT's national framework. Table 2.2 shows Barnett's categorization between operational and academic competence. He agrees that this is a simplistic approach, but it is one that is most useful in trying to unravel the demands and requirements of the ILT.

Table 2.2   Barnett's two rival versions of competence

	Operational Competence	Academic Competence
1. Epistemology	know how	know that
2. Situations	define pragmatically	define by intellectual field
3. Focus	outcomes	propositions
4. Transferability	metaoperations	metacognition
5. Learning	experiential	propositional
6. Communication	strategic	disciplinary
7. Evaluation	economic	truthfulness
8. Value Orientation	economic survival	disciplinary strength
9. Boundary Conditions	organizational norms	norms of intellectual field
10. Critique	for better practical effectiveness	for better cognitive understanding

The ILT requires evidence of competence, a type of evidence that reflects a certain sort of competence, a competence based on an 'operational' view of competence. By comparing the nature of CPD requirements within the national framework to Barnett's categorization of competence, it is possible to identify and construct a model of evidence that reflects competence to be a narrowly conceived aim, which will not encourage the academic community to engage in the development of good practice in learning and teaching, but will require academics merely to demonstrate a more effective way of doing things. Thus, they will not be engaged in the more academic competence, which relates to the understanding and underpinning principles and values that go to making practice more effective. For example, the statement about required documentation for CPD starts: 'The Institute accepts and strongly endorses the need for an appropriate mix of subject-based and pedagogical elements in members' professional development records. Such elements should clearly reflect the different roles, contexts and teaching responsibilities of individuals and documentation should normally contain a range of evidence drawn from a variety of sources.'

It recommends that examples of evidence may be collected from a variety of sources including descriptions, evaluations and reflections on formal and informal learning aimed at maintaining, updating and upgrading knowledge, expertise and professional practice. The evidence collected and collated must then be submitted as a professional development record (PDR), which should place emphasis on outcomes and the application of learning; in addition to this the PDR will be assessed against national outcomes.

What is evident here is that the emphasis is on the demonstrations of outcomes, suggesting that the ideologies on which the creation of the PDR and its assessment are based are outcomes-orientated, in line with 'operationally orientated competence'. Clearly what is being expected here is the type of outcomes that demonstrate changes in operational situations or in situations affecting operations. Competence is seen as a function of an ability to control outcomes or to compensate for them. This is reflected in some of the suggested types of admissible evidence, for example:

- evaluated activities aimed at the improvement of learning methods and teaching performance;
- action-research and evaluation of individual's own teaching and assessment methods;
- examples of the development of new learning resources or innovative curriculum design;
- relevant management/leadership activities of direct relevance to learning and teaching (eg preparation for subject review, mentoring of new academic staff).

All of these examples are 'outcomes'-led and 'focus' on what Barnett has termed the distinction between pragmatic results and cognitive offerings. A similar argument may be put towards what one might term critique. The ILT has an expectation that applicants will demonstrate their reflective capacity in the five broad areas stated in the national framework. Critical reflection is discussed in detail in Chapter 4, where it takes the discussion beyond the immediate concerns of the ILT and considers how reflection may be used most effectively in future professional development frameworks. The purpose of raising the issue of critique and reflection here is to contextualize its role in terms of ILT demands. Within the present discussion, critique is taken and examined in terms of operational competence, ie that of better practical effectiveness and academic competence, rather than that of a better cognitive understanding.

The main aim of the CPD requirements is to maintain good standing within the professional body of the ILT. Its demands, as have previously been stated, are to demonstrate 'professional competence and the enhancement or extension of professional competence', through reflection on evidence collected to meet stated outcomes.

This suggests that the type of reflection expected is intended to bring about greater effectiveness in learning and teaching. This raises a question that needs consideration: if the anticipated change is to occur through reflection, how can preconceived outcomes help greater effectiveness? For if academics know the outcomes on which they are to be assessed they will operationalize their 'critique' to be reflective and demonstrate the required 'greater effectiveness' without actually changing anything. Surely the type of critique that should be demanded is one that demonstrates academic competence, that leads to a better cognitive understanding.

If teaching and learning are to improve one needs to have more than an operational understanding of 'greater effectiveness'. Lecturers need to know more than *when* something does or does not work in a learning environment; they need to know *why* it has worked or not worked. This relies on understanding the concepts, ideas and theories that are related to various aspects of teaching and learning within a given discipline. To reach the level of understanding may well include reflection, even if the nature of reflection is contained within a single discipline. The reflection however needs to include understanding of *why* and *how* operational success and failures occur. Here again Barnett's distinction helps the discussion. He states: 'Academic critique is reflection orientated towards understanding better the already existing understanding. On the other hand, critique in the operational sense is an understanding that enables us "to go on" with greater confidence' (p 166).

At present this well describes the type of reflection the ILT expects from portfolio material: reflection that shows improved performance based on outcomes. It must be said that there is merit in this type of improvement, and Schön clearly demonstrates this in his arguments related to knowledge-in-use. However, if long-term change in learning and teaching is to happen, the nature of the demands as laid out by the ILT needs to be reconsidered and possibly reflect a more academic view of critique, one that demonstrates a clear underpinning of cognitive understanding of the discipline being represented.

Using the categories of operational and academic competence helps to demonstrate the direction of the ILT's view to development. Yet if academics are to improve their teaching and support of learning they need to know and appreciate what constitutes learning and how this might be enhanced through their teaching. This requires engaging with the cognitive elements of teaching and learning, not just trying to improve teaching through operational practice.

Surgery, vaccine or palliative care?

Earlier in this chapter I introduced a medical analogy as a means of understanding how the demands of the ILT might be perceived. Let us return to this analogy as I try to summarize the issues and dilemmas now facing academics and the ILT.

First, is there an 'illness' in teaching and learning support within higher education, or is it a perceived illness? There is no doubt that good, bad and indifferent practice is in existence in higher education. But we need evidence of exactly what the illness is and where it lurks before anything can be done about it. After all, surgeons do not go blindly into surgery; they conduct exploratory courses of action first. If the ILT was set up to cut out bad or ineffective practice, then surely it too should conduct exploratory courses of action into the perceived bad practice, prior to imposing a form of action. Or is it more a case that the demands as specified in the national framework are actually aimed at providing a vaccine for the higher education community, in respect of teaching and learning? In other words, if every new lecturer to the academic community has to go through an induction programme that gives entry to the ILT then this gives new academics a *vaccine* against poor or ineffective teaching and learning support practices. The hope is that they will transfer whatever skills they have been introduced to into their own teaching and learning environments, thus stemming the flow of bad or ineffective practice. Here the vaccine attempts to prevent the illness from occurring in the first instance. By demanding that individuals then remain in good standing through a CPD portfolio that has to be submitted at regular intervals the vaccine is given a booster shot to ensure that the illness remains at bay or, at the very least, should the illness attack, that its effect will be minimal.

What of those already well established in the higher education community? What kind of treatment is being prescribed for them? Within my analogy it would seem that they are being encouraged to have palliative care, on the basis that long-established academics may well find the whole process of applying for membership burdensome, and also possibly accepting that they will not change their ways, and thus have no real hope for any change. A 'fast-track' entry system has been established in the first instance, but as with any palliative care the premise is that there is no cure; care is continually re-evaluated and reconsidered. The ILT's treatment of experienced academics is no different. Having gained membership through fast track, which will only be available for a limited number of years, academics will have to be re-evaluated and will have to demonstrate 'good standing'. Should they not meet the standard at this point, there does not at present seem to be any indication as to what their future will then be with respect to the ILT. Will this be a termination of membership and hence of academic careers, or will it be that a different form of palliative care is designed for these individuals, or will a new form of vaccine be developed for them?

It is interesting that in all of this the individual features only marginally. It also portrays a rather bleak picture of the demands of the ILT. Maybe it is that the original vision of the ILT as prescribed by Dearing and then developed by the Booth committee has gradually been eroded in the development and establishment of the ILT's mission and national framework. This may well be an important factor in why the language and direction of the prescription from the ILT has caused such great consternation in the higher education community. Competency-based systems and prescriptive language based on generic norms and values don't bode well with those who essentially come from a diversity of backgrounds and disciplines. That is not to say that academics within these disciplines and diverse backgrounds don't wish to engage in the discourse or dialogues related to teaching and learning in their respective fields. It is more a question of making the demands for membership reflect the diversity of the higher education community. The setting up of discipline-based centres will help considerably. It will be interesting to see how and in what guises these centres develop and the possible impact they may have on teaching and learning support within the designated disciplines.

Dilemmas of the ILT demands

I have put forward the argument, based on evidence from the higher education community and those associated with the development of teaching and learning support within the sector, that the demands of the ILT are over-prescriptive and too generic in their approach. The argument has also suggested that, by taking an operational view of competence and looking at 'practical outcomes' based on a type of reflection that only requires the individual to engage with elements of what works and does not work, the ILT has in effect ignored the values and principles of many academics. The overall effect of this is for academics to feel that the demands are over-burdensome and difficult to engage with, and that this extra work often deters them from the research that institutions actually want them to engage in. This essentially brings us back full circle to the teaching–research nexus.

The ILT was set up, as stated earlier, to promote and enhance the status of teaching. However, the way in which it has set out its functions, demands and expectations appears to be working against its mission statement. Surely this is not what the higher education community wants. It is certainly not what Dearing envisaged when he recommended the creation of the ILT.

It also seems evident that, as more institutions are accredited and as each accredited institution will reflect its own diversity and expectations with its accredited courses, the demands of the ILT will in effect be interpreted in a variety of combinations and permutations. The extent to which these combinations and permutations actually create a more effective teaching and learning community needs monitoring and researching.

If one considers the demands of the ILT in terms of the requirements set out by a 'professional body', it is acceptable to say that these demands are right and fitting. Yet, what is missing from the demands appears to be the recognition that most academics are professionals already and have had their professional status endorsed by their own disciplined-based professional body. Where does this leave the ILT and the academic? Certainly the answer to this question is key to any future professional development framework that the higher education community will engage in.

The dilemma can be summarized as follows:

- Raising the status of teaching and learning through an imposed professional body ignores the fact that many academics already see themselves as accredited professionals.
- Imposing generic demands related to teaching and learning practices is actually increasing the distinction between teaching and research rather than narrowing it.
- Having operational-based competencies moves away from the premise of encouraging academics to engage with the reasons why teaching and learning can be improved and enhanced.
- Evidence of competence based on operational outcomes encourages academics to write and produce work that meets the assessment criteria, rather than seriously engaging with the issues and problems associated with improving teaching and learning support.

Concluding comments

Within this chapter I have attempted to explore and contextualize the demands and functions of the ILT, by introducing the notions of the professional body, the professional within it and the demands such a body might expect from its members. In order to compare the mission and vision of the ILT with its demands on its membership I have looked at and discussed the terms and language used in the ILT demands. This has led to a consideration of competence and requirements.

Through this discussion and exploration it can be seen that the ILT has merit in being a professional body, and as such it wishes to raise the status and standards of its target audience by setting very clear aims, objectives and demands. This is an acceptable argument if we assume that the ILT is a professional body, but this assumption has raised many issues related to the community it is trying to serve. The medical analogy used to describe the demands of the ILT has shown that both it and the higher education community have first to decide what might constitute the illness, and as a consequence of this diagnosis establish the nature of the treatment that may be required, and how the treatment is to be administered.

What is clear is that the demands are over-prescriptive in some areas and that the framework as it stands is over-complex and unclear in its direction. For future demands the ILT will have to consider investigating or at the very least establishing ways in which it can identify areas of weakness so that treatments can match the ailment, rather than producing a mass immunization programme that individuals follow but do not actually engage in.

Despite these assertions, dilemmas and statements, it is clear that the ILT is here to stay and that individuals are joining the professional body, whatever their demands are and however they wish to meet them. This in itself is posing an interesting question for the higher education community and creating a dilemma for the academic: to join or not to join, that is the question.

The demands of the ILT, now or in the future, need to be considered in the wider context of the role of professional development within the higher education community. Central to this consideration is the role the individual and the institution have to play in ensuring good practice and high standards of teaching and learning.

3

The changing role of professional development in higher education

Introduction

Having considered the role and implications of the ILT in the previous chapter, it is now necessary to examine the role of professional development within the context of the ILT and higher education more generally. This chapter gives a description and overview of the role, concepts and issues related to professional development in higher education. It discusses the relationship between learning from learning, different ways of learning and knowing, and professional development.

Professional development has many aspects and facets to its name. Within higher education much of the discussion relates to learning, whether this be life-long learning, organizational learning or discipline-based learning. Higher education concentrates on learning, both of students and of academics. It is therefore right and fitting that the fundamental premise within the chapter is that professional development is closely allied to the learning cycle. From this premise consideration is given to the impact and influence professional development approaches may have within institutions. These will include administrative procedures and commitments to programmes, support networks from institutions and senior colleagues, and resource implications. The conclusion will aim to identify underpinning criteria for a framework and rationale of professional development in higher education.

Issues, role, concepts and practices of professional development

Professional education is concerned with three main aspects of development, namely the professional knowledge base, competence in professional action and the development of reflection. Yet, one of the paradoxes of professional education is that practitioners are encouraged to develop a critical awareness of the context of their practice. This awareness includes the problems of their clients, whether they be patients or students, while at the same time the notion is perpetuated that the professional practitioner is an autonomous free-thinking agent. If this is the case, one has to ask the question: how do practitioners learn their practitioner role?

This is a pertinent question in higher education as we enter the new millennium, particularly when statutory requirements related to the development of learning and teaching skills are being placed on the practitioner. Practitioners may consider themselves to be research chemists, psychologists or economists by definition in the first instance, not teachers, yet they are being asked to be excellent teacher practitioners. This reflects Schön's argument of the rigour-or-relevance dilemma: 'What aspiring practitioners need most to learn, professional schools seem least able to teach. The schools' version of the dilemma is rooted, like the practitioners', in an underlying and largely unexamined epistemology of professional practice, a model of professional knowledge institutionally embedded in curriculum and arrangements for research and practice' (1987: 8). He goes on to argue that modern research universities are premised on technical rationality that presents first the science, then the application and finally a practicum, in which students are presumed to learn to apply research-based knowledge to everyday practice. The implications of this are considerable for the situation higher education now finds itself in, ie a group of academics trained as described by Schön, but expected to demonstrate 'good practice'. Increasingly the question that needs to be asked of practitioners in higher education is: what is the practitioner role of the academic at the present time and how does this relate to professional development programmes in higher education?

This is a very emotive question, which produces many differing responses, each related to the position, philosophy and political stance taken. Yet, the reality is that although the perceptions of the practitioner in higher education are multi-variant, the expectations of government and higher education itself are not always synonymous, but polar.

The means by which institutions or governments, whether national, regional or local, set out to control the activities of the professions are many and diverse, as are the motives for seeking such control. What many of them have in common is a focus on education and training and on certification. That is the condition under which specialized (and marketable) qualifications are awarded. Professional development in higher education is no different, with many institutions currently developing and or awarding certification at various levels for learning and teaching in higher education. The main aim is to help academic practitioners meet the requirements of the ILT and give status to learning and teaching through certification. This may indeed meet the criteria for claiming teaching knowledge, but it does not mean a better or more informed teaching community in higher education, nor does it fill the professional development requirements of all academics within higher education.

It is pertinent at this juncture to identify what is meant by professional development. Professional development is a dynamic process that spans one's entire career in a profession, from preparation and induction to completion and retirement. This view is based on the assumption that any successful professional development relies on a relationship related to the individual's work environment and that individual's perception of his or her role within it. Figure 3.1 shows the relationship between professional development and the individual within an institution.

Figure 3.1   Professional development and the individual

Central to this conceptualization of professional development is the position of each of the constituent parts, and the effect each has on the individual. It is important for this discussion to consider each aspect, and then move on to how these aspects affect and are linked to notions of learning and professional education.

Learning from learning

For university academics, it is the case that contact with the teaching and learning situation on an almost daily basis has always contributed to the development of their academic and pedagogic knowledge and skills. This being the case we can assume that practitioners have been involved in personal development and learning by the nature of their positions and job. Equally, professional development is part of learning, and studying the subject and related issues is a privilege for those involved in education and educational studies. Yet, in a learning society we are forced to ask questions relating to professional development and its role in learning. A consequence of the Dearing Report has been the need for the higher education sector to consider and enter the debate about learning from learning and how this equates to scholarship. It is suggested here that 'learning from learning' is a key facet of development. This point is strongly argued by Becher (1996). In this context professional development is seen as having its central concern with the promotion and support of learning, not only of the students, but also for the academics themselves in their own personal and professional development.

Research has shown that the ways in which teachers think about teaching substantially influences the approaches to learning adopted by students (Prosser and Trigwell, 1999). Research has also shown that academics' view of the nature of knowledge and the relationship of that knowledge to their teaching influences the extent to which they are prepared to innovate, and learn from their teaching (Brew and Wright, 1990). If learning is taken as a process of construction (Entwistle, 1997; Biggs, 1996; Prosser and Trigwell, 1999), as being about creating knowledge rather than simply absorbing it, then an alternative perspective can be given to the academic learning from his or her research and teaching.

The concept of learning can be viewed as developing a personal understanding of a phenomenon, in this case teaching, research, scholarship and the links between them. The implication of this is that teaching needs to take account of how individuals develop their conceptions as well as the conceptions that are being developed. Key in this argument is that the academic has to understand that the relationship between teaching and research is dynamic and context-driven. What is important to the argument is that if such a process does not occur then that individual is not engaged in developing and learning. This would suggest that if academics are to be learners, and learning given value, then learning opportunities that provide access and progression (in this case to teaching/learning programmes through professional development) have to be actively and reflexively engaged in. Edwards (1997) quite correctly emphasizes that there has been a shift in focus from the provision of education as training to one that focuses on the learner and learning. Thus he argues that the discourse of lifelong learning has shifted to one of reflexive challenges, one that requires the professional to learn and understand the learning that has taken place. This is a key facet when we come to examine the role of assessment in Chapter 4.

Different ways of knowing and learning

Ways of learning have a significant role to play in professional development. It is essential that the structure of knowledge and alternative approaches to learning are given a more constructive framework in which to operate. The literature on learning is vast, and a review of such literature indicates that the various dimensions of learning can be polarized in two categories, those of concrete–abstract and reflective–active. Such a polarization is a useful way of considering the type of learning that may contribute to professional learning and the role that professional development has in that learning.

Examining the first of the two polarities, that of concrete–abstract, allows us to consider how knowledge is perceived. This is a key element in the discussion of learning within a professional domain, where one aspect of a professional's world by definition relates to his or her knowledge base. Knowledge can be seen to have one pole that is dominated by the abstract, analytical approach usually associated with academic research, where the learning focuses on objectivity and demands high levels of specialization from the individual, who takes pride in claiming that such knowledge is 'value-free'. In contrast, at the other end of this continuum, knowledge is based on the concrete experience, what is learnt from contexts, relationships and valuing communities.

In order to conceptualize professional learning in this way it is necessary to consider the elements that may affect the role of the individual within the learning context. Three areas will be considered, which have been derived from Lortie (1975). They focus on the organizational, associational and professional elements of the academic's development. The first aspect, organizational, relates to the role of the academic within the structural and policy-making framework of the state; the second considers the academic's response to issues of pay and conditions of work; the third relates to the academic's attempts to promote his or her role, autonomy and image.

Professional development is about learning and modes of learning. At present most modes of professional development in higher education are shaped by the social structures in which they are located and by the influence of historical traditions of learning. What is missing from this is an element that allows individual practitioners to focus on professional self-understanding and aims, as well as on the actual developments in education, work, markets and career developments of the members of the profession, in this case members of the academic community. Becher (1996) suggests that theories about professions and models of professionalization fail to deal adequately with the role of the state, government and legislation. Giddens's view reinforces this argument by suggesting that 'if a structuralist and post-structuralist conceptualisation is taken where patterning is considered as an intersection of presence and absence, where underlying codes have to be inferred from surface manifestations, a clear view of the government's position can be seen' (1995: 37). The role of government should not be underestimated in the changes that are being imposed on professional development within higher education.

Lifelong learning

Lifelong learning can be considered as being involved with the development of a range of interactions between educational institutions and their host communities, in this case academics, students and higher education institutions (HEIs). All are, or should be, concerned to develop a learning community, where learning is valued, for both the teacher and the student. For this to occur, the professional development of those who facilitate learning at all levels must be recognized.

At the level of individual academics, systems and authorities should offer opportunities for them to participate in professional development work in preparation for lifelong learning, and therefore help them to develop the concept of lifelong learning for themselves.

The premise here is that the provision of some forms of lifelong learning is heavily dependent on the skills, knowledge and professional competency of the teaching profession, rather than the elements of reflexive learning. The challenge will be to extend and broaden the frameworks of teaching and learning activities in higher education to incorporate a more reflexive approach to learning. The academic as well as the student should be involved in such learning.

The development of a reflexive professional is a long-term process, which is progressive and goes over the working lifetime of a professional. It is planned, and prioritized. Lifelong learning, however, goes beyond the *working life* of a professional. At present, professional development is only orientated towards the working lifetime of a professional (in this case the academic), although professional development should be thought of as only one element of lifelong learning. If such a premise is to be accepted, there is a need to consider the role of learning for the professional and how this may affect the role of teaching in higher education.

Professional learning

Professional learning is a key aspect in any discussion related to professional development. Work by the Carnegie Foundation, and in particular Ernest Boyer, has drawn attention to professional learning within the academic community. Boyer suggested: 'All faculty members, throughout their careers, should themselves remain students. As scholars they must continue to learn and be seriously and continuously engaged in the expanding intellectual world' (1987: 10). Further work by Lynton and Elman (1987) urged that special attention be given to the scholar's role in a university's responsibility for the application and the utilization of knowledge. It is for this reason that a great deal of emphasis has been placed on learning, and the individual's role in learning within professional development, throughout this book. Chapter 6 takes up the theme of professional learning though the example of Richard Feynman, the eminent physicist.

Teaching and learning

A significant amount of research (for example Bolam, 1987; Dean, 1996) has examined the role of professional development and the professional, but the role of teachers' learning has not always been made explicit and explained. Professional development in higher education is now being used as a way of improving the quality of learning and teaching of the academic. In many instances this is happening through the engaging of academics in a form of reflexive professional development, thus trying to instil a culture of lifelong learning.

Opportunities for individuals to extend their knowledge base, skills and teaching activities are being provided, as recommended in *Higher Education for the 21st Century*. The document states that 'all institutions of higher education give high priority to developing and implementing learning and teaching strategies which focus on the promotion of students' learning' (DfEE, 1998: 19). Despite these statements this remains a contentious issue, with research being given a greater importance and status than teaching, by the presence of the Research Assessment Exercise (RAE). This dilemma is acknowledged here, but is not the focus of the discussion.

Practice, in this case teaching, does not happen in a vacuum. It depends on a variety of social, political and ideological contexts. The practice of teaching in higher education and the role of learning for the professional academic are equally dependent on the whole educational context, particularly at this time when universities are facing periods of rapid change. Consideration must be given to the learning environment of the professional, in preparation for the imposed change.

Research has shown (Elton, 1992; Rowland, 1999) that development and reaction to change are enhanced when the importance of the working environment is considered. Garrett (1997) makes a significant point when he suggests that the development process must not be alienated from the context of practice. The context may vary across institutions and within schools or faculties, but is influenced by both formal and informal, internally and externally imposed, structures and strategies, such as the ILT and the RAE. For higher education, this means considering how teaching is going to affect the role of learning for the academic in the pursuit of new knowledge and the teacher (who is often the same person) applying his or her theoretical knowledge to a teaching situation. As members of a university, individuals are expected not only to practise an art or science, but also to act as a 'professor' of knowledge (Garrett, 1997: 49). If this is the case, are the learning needs the same, and can one be classified as 'learning' and the other as 'development of skills', or is one aspect connected implicitly to the other?

The resolution of such questions rests on how we perceive the need to change the academic, and what the perceived changes entail in terms of professional development and learning. The present climate in higher education suggests that all new university academics will have to obtain some formal or accredited teaching qualification. The nature of this qualification is open to interpretation and discussion.

This presents us with a dilemma. Should we be designing induction courses for academics to develop basic teaching skills, thus applying a 'deficit' model of professional development? This suggests that the new academic does not possess these basic teaching skills and therefore has to be inducted to them. If this is the case we are viewing academics as objects rather than subjects of their professional growth (Huberman, 1995). What we should be striving for, if teaching standards in HE are to improve and change, is to understand how academics learn and change, and the role teaching plays in that change.

So why should academics develop their knowledge in relation to teaching and learning, and be motivated to become 'good teachers'? It is clear that personal and institutional influences affect academics' motivation to participate in professional education activities. The transaction between the individual and the external factors contribute to a state of motivational energy to engage in continual professional development. The factors that affect academics' participation can be grouped into personal or situational categories. Much of the research in this area suggests that reasons for participation or lack of participation can be aligned with personal factors, which contribute to and influence their level of motivation. Rowland highlights the issue of motivation in relation to the pressure for academics to embrace the notion of good teaching. When talking of the academic, he suggests: 'On the other side of the battle-lines are the workers in academic departments who are under pressure to be more research productive. At best, they view those in these [staff development] units as providing a service to help them teach. At worst, they ignore them as lacking academic credibility and being irrelevant to the real intellectual tasks of academic life' (Rowland *et al*, 1998: 134).

This highlights a significant problem area for higher education, and introduces an interesting concept at the same time. The problem relates to work-based learning, in that new programmes for change are being conducted at work, and the courses are often run by other academics or staff developers. The concept is an interesting one, as evidence relating to teacher professional learning and development within the workplace is frequently absent from the research literature. What is needed is an understanding of the relationship between specific dimensions of the higher education workplace environment and the academic within that framework. The role of professional education should play a key part in understanding the participatory elements of course design within a workplace situation.

Professional education

Professional education can be directed through three main models, that of the 'apprenticeship' or 'pre-technocratic', 'technocratic' and 'post-technocratic'. Each model has a distinct focus and is driven by different ideals and concepts of development. Trying to establish the model that exists at present, as well as trying to suggest ways forward for the future, requires an examination of the three models.

Apprenticeship or pre-technocratic model of professional education

Professional education within this model takes place largely on the job but some interaction may be given through attending day courses or block periods of time in other education or training institutions. The curriculum is mainly composed of the acquisition of 'cookbook' knowledge embodied in practical manuals or tips for the job, with mastery being gained through practical routines. Within this model much of the on-the-job learning and instruction is given by peers or experienced practitioners, although individuals may be introduced to outside speakers and subject specialists.

This model is more often found in initial training than in continuing professional development. The primary focus of the apprenticeship model is learning about professional requirements and competencies, many of which have been identified by external agencies. Many of the courses at present on offer to new academics appear to match the apprenticeship/pre-technocratic model of professional education. The new academic has to follow a course of initial training often leading to a postgraduate certificate in education, or certification of some form that is acceptable to the ILT.

Technocratic model

In recent years this has become the dominant model of professional education for a large number of professionals and professional bodies. This model categorizes development into three main elements:

1.   development and transmission of a systematic body of knowledge;
2.   the interpretation and application of knowledge to practice;
3.   supervised practice in selected placements.

This type of model requires most of the training and education to occur in an institution of higher education, where control of the courses is in the hands of the institution. National bodies may select and accredit institutions for these courses. However, curriculum content and delivery, as well as final assessment, both academically and practically, whether this be competence based or not, are largely left to the institutions to develop and administer. Increasingly with higher education institutions gaining accredited status from the ILT, new and experienced academics will be involved in this type of professional education model. This should cause some apprehension as the model can be regarded as having significant weaknesses, despite it offering the individual the opportunity to develop personally and professionally.

The weakness lies in the fact that each institution will interpret concepts of professional competence, knowledge base required and approaches to teaching and learning strategies in a different way. Such variations in requirements raise issues about the level of competence and how quality assurance is maintained. Secondly, the model is thought to fragment the overall learning situation, by forcing learning into discrete and unrelated parts, including disjunction between theory and practice. The model is based on what Schön (1983) describes as the 'technical rationality model', that is, a view of both professionalism and professional education that fails to reflect the nature of professional knowledge and action and the ways in which professionals actually develop their practice.

These concerns have often been voiced in higher education, where there has been a continued sense that real knowledge is scientific knowledge (Barnett, 1994: 14) and that propositional knowledge is overvalued (Eraut, 1994). As a consequence of this persistent rhetoric, professional education has tended to assume the same perspective, in part because the growth of a profession has depended to a significant extent on the development of a knowledge base.

Within professional education it is an underlying assumption that such education should enable the individual to develop a variety of knowledge bases, including conceptual knowledge, procedural knowledge and personal knowledge, and to recognize and address the impact these have on individuals and their development. It is the understanding, interpretation and application of such knowledge bases that are important to professional practice. One purpose of professional education is to enable these assumptions to be brought to the surface so that their implications for professional practice can be explored. This process includes professional self-management or 'the thinking involved in directing one's own behaviour and controlling one's engagement in learning' (Eraut, 1994: 115).

If professional education, in the form of imposed programmes related to teaching and learning strategies, is to be effective in higher education, those developing such strategies have to be aware of what Schön (1989) describes as the difference between 'espoused theories' or the explicit theories that explain professional behaviour, and 'theories in use' or the implicit theories that actually determine behaviour. It is implicit theories that are key to the discussion. Attitudes, values and beliefs that influence how individuals interpret their professional knowledge govern implicit theories. Research in the field of teacher education has shown that programmes rarely challenge existing assumptions about teaching and learning, a consequence of which is that there is little attempt to change teaching styles (Tann, 1993; Day, 1999; Rowland, 1999).

Such research cannot be ignored when considering the nature and context of training programmes in higher education. Inducting and training new lecturers into the art of teaching is a skilful task. Research about individual perception into teaching should be a key consideration both before and during the development of programmes connected to teaching and learning strategies for higher education lecturers. This is particularly so, as research (Nicholls, 1997, 2000) shows that many academics already have personal constructs that put teaching as low priority and not a main criterion for promotion within the academic world. The implication of these findings for developing courses is and should be significant. If new lecturers come to imposed programmes already holding strong preconceived ideas in relation to the role and value of teaching and learning, and these conceptions are not synonymous with where they think their learning should be going, it is then possible to draw the conclusion that the professional development programme being offered is going to be a non-starter.

For professional education to be meaningful, careful consideration is required of the relationships between the various participants involved, and of the preconceived ideas and values that are brought to the programmes. This will lead to the development of a more effective and workable partnership. It should reflect the processes by which we expect new lecturers to acquire the knowledge, skills and values that will improve their teaching and the general service they provide to their students. Lecturers need to become critically aware of how and why their assumptions shape the way they see themselves and others. It is only by reconstructing this framework that it becomes possible for lecturers to become more inclusive and discriminating in the integration of their experiences and thus begin to act on the understanding they have gained. This process is essential for professional practice. In a world that is changing so rapidly, and higher education can't be removed from that change, it is inevitable that the experiences encountered by academics will be unpredictable. Learning from experiences is essential if continuing professional development and lifelong learning are to take place (Taylor, 1997: 43).

The above argument is thus suggesting that professional education should enable academics to recognize their preconceptions and develop their personal knowledge in such a way as to recognize the impact on practice, in this case teaching, it might have. Professional education itself then must be aware of its aims and intentions. Taylor suggests that 'a gap is caused through the lack of attention in professional education to the dynamic relationship between propositional knowledge and personal knowledge and the contribution it makes' (1997: 39).

Developing a critical awareness in this way is one of the paradoxes of professional education. Developing a critical awareness of the context of practice and the problems associated with their clients (in this case their students) while at the same time perpetuating the notion that professional practitioners are autonomous, free-thinking agents, leads to questioning another aspect of professional education: exactly how do practitioners learn their practitioner role? For indeed a profession, or discipline, not only has practice, but it also has a theory of action in which that practice can become a reproducible, valid technique. This process is professional development. It is a form of growth, both personal and professional. These two aspects are part of the same concept. All too often they are discussed and exemplified as separate phenomena. Research indicates otherwise (Nicholls, 2000; Day, 1999; Taylor, 1997). Professional development and personal growth can and often do occur simultaneously, because professional development is not simply a matter of conferences and courses to attend, but a participative activity that requires critical awareness.

Recognizing some of the problems and weakness of the technocratic model has led to the development of the third model, post-technocratic. This model is still in the developmental stages, but it is gaining ground and importance in the assessment of professional competence by both external agencies and governments.

Post-technocratic professional education

The distinctive feature of this model is the acquisition of professional competence. The competencies are developed through practice and reflection on practice in a situation in which the individual has access to a skilled or experienced practitioner who acts as a mentor or coach. The environment in which development and learning are to occur is called the practicum, and it is the essential element binding the learning together through the professional tutor and practice tutor. All elements of this model focus on professional practice and competence within that practice.

The model has a number of issues and weaknesses attached to it, owing to its being composed from a potentially disparate set of elements, which arise from a difference in opinions from different professions and their associated practices. The consequence of this has been that various forms of the competence-based model of professional education have emerged. Two main versions seem to be dominating present discussions. Both are worthy of consideration as they have implications for the long-term models of professional development and professional education of new and experienced academics in higher education.

The first version of the competence model relates to the identification and description of a range of discrete competencies, usually described in behavioural terms. These are then developed and assessed, primarily through practice settings (Tuxworth, 1989). The second version still concentrates on the practicum, but does not concentrate quite so much on discrete competencies as on the general development of a capacity for critical reflection in and on action, as the key to continuing professional growth (McNamara, 1990).

Both these models need consideration. They challenge those involved with professional education to consider the knowledge base from which competencies are derived and formulated by a given profession. They also force assessors to consider the issues related to how individuals learn and how that can be demonstrated within a competency model. Here lies a serious issue for the future of professional development in higher education.

The model lies on epistemologically distinct aspects, namely the behaviourist approaches that have been favoured by the competency movement and the interpretative theories of thinking and action that underpin the concept of reflection and reflective practice. Where does this leave the question of professional development of the new academic? Here issues related to the design, type and nature of professional development courses have to be addressed. For example, how will the course allow for the integration of knowledge and action, so that practicum is both effective and efficient for the individual engaged with the course? How will this model be adapted for experienced members of staff wishing to engage in continual professional development? Will the courses and competencies within them be continuous or will they be distinct at different levels of engagement?

It is not clear at present with the ILT if professional development is going to remain at initial level. Discussions are already taking place about the continual professional development of academics, but there is very little evidence to date as to how these models of development, both initial and continuing, are to be integrated, and from which competence model they will be derived. One thing that is interesting and will need to be monitored is that most competency models have begun with initial training before progressing to continual development. Will this be the same for higher education? Despite there being no claim made that the present type of professional education new academics are engaging in is to be associated with a competency model, much of the assessment that is taking place relates to levels of competence. These levels are at present implicit to the development programme, for example peer observation and assessment of teaching sessions. How long will it be before the ILT states the competencies required and the means by which these will be assessed formally, thus ensuring a common assessment process for all academics and institutions?

Concluding comments

Much of this chapter has considered the role and issues related to professional development. At the centre of the discussion has been the premise that learning and learning from learning are keys to success. However, it has also highlighted areas that at present do not necessarily help with the notion of learning from learning, whether this is thought of as professional learning, teaching and learning or lifelong learning. Key to the issues raised have been the way professional learning is constituted and the way the models of professional education have shaped and are shaping courses for new and experienced academics in higher education.

The debate has concentrated on how knowledge is viewed and the effect this has on the types and role professional education has to play in professional development. Each model has it strengths and weaknesses and each can and does have an influence on the nature and context of professional development programmes. However, the competency-based model has been considered as having a significant impact on present and more importantly future approaches to development programmes.

Issues concerning competence remain at the heart of long-standing debates about what constitutes professionalism, including issues related to rationality and reflection. Enmeshed in all of this has been the assessment of professional competence. Some versions of the model have made assessment implicit to its nature, whereas other versions have made competence levels explicit and have required an entry profile. A consequence of these debates has been the call that a competency model that is explicit in its level of competence is required to make a profession more efficient and effective.

A cautionary note was brought out at the end of this chapter: despite some of the claims of a competency model, we should give serious consideration to the nature of the professional development programmes being suggested, some of which appear to be implicitly adopting a competency-based model, as developments in higher education might not in themselves provide the solutions to improved teaching and learning in higher education.

Three major issues need to be given serious consideration before any future courses or programmes are accredited:

1. What does competence in teaching and learning in higher education mean?
2. What are the competencies required by the academic profession?
3. How are competencies best developed and assessed in higher education?

Professional education and the role it has within the professional development of the academic must remain high on the agenda for both academic institutions and the ILT. Collaboration is an essential element to successful development of future professional development programmes, ones that offer individuals the ability to learn and be reflective about their learning, as well as be accountable for the type of development they have engaged in.

4

Assessment, reflection and professional development

Introduction

Reflection and learning are key elements of any professional development programme, and yet increasingly these particular elements are being assessed. The rationale for this assessment and the criteria by which it is to be carried out are not clear. This chapter examines the relationship between the assessment through the ILT of new academics for the purposes of teaching and learning, and the values that academic institutions propagate. It argues that the current assessment practices are incompatible with the goals of the reflective practitioner as a means to the higher-quality teaching, learning, scholarship and critical analysis to which most academics would subscribe.

At present, assessment of professional development within higher education revolves around the demands of the ILT. However, as academics we need to examine such assessment practices to see if they are compatible with our academic ideals and more generally the goals of higher education. Throughout this book it has been argued that the academic has to identify with his or her own learning. If assessment of this learning is to occur, the assessment procedures used must reflect the nature of that learning, as well as promote that learning. Meaningful learning and reflective practice are more likely to occur when new and experienced academics engage with the pedagogic practice of their disciplines for its own sake, not for that of an external demand.

The chapter identifies the main reasons and purposes for assessment of professional development and discusses some of the fundamental issues and problems associated with such assessment practices. The discussion is placed in the context of learning processes and the role reflection has to play within that process. The discussion does not focus on or relate to the assessment methods themselves, as these are less important than the role assessment has within teaching and learning programmes related to professional development.

Purpose of assessment

All forms of assessment provide estimates of the individual's current status and should primarily be concerned with providing guidance and feedback to the learner. The position taken here is that feedback that creates a learning environment is the central and most important function of assessment in relation to professional development. The results of assessment can be used for judgemental and for developmental purposes. Figure 4.1 shows how assessment can be characterized to show the continuum from judgemental to developmental. In this context developmental assessment is concerned with improving academics' learning; this is directly related to and founded on trust between individuals and their senior colleagues or designated mentors. Judgemental assessment is concerned with licence to proceed and allied to accountability and accreditation.

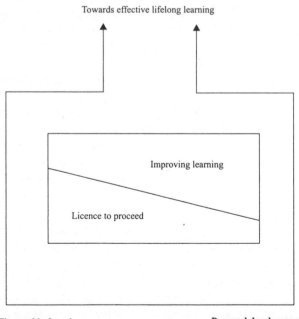

Figure 4.1   Assessment and development

Establishing reasons why academics might need to be assessed requires an understanding of the purposes of assessment. The general purposes in relation to academics and their professional development can be summarized in the following ways:

- provide feedback to improve learning;
- motivate individuals;
- diagnose strengths and weaknesses;
- help develop skills of self-assessment;
- provide a profile of what has been learnt or developed;
- pass or fail individuals;
- provide licence to proceed;
- provide licence to practise;
- predict success in future employment.

The above list can be divided into two main purposes: one related to feedback and one related to accreditation and accountability.

The first is intended to improve the quality of teaching and learning through reflection and reflective practice. New and experienced academics engage in the problems and discourses of their disciplines' pedagogic practices, and are given encouragement, response and feedback on what they do, as appropriate, with a view to them becoming more reflective as teachers and reflective practitioners. This is developmental or formative assessment, a type of assessment that allows participants to learn from their assessed performance.

The second concerns accreditation of knowledge or performance. Here new academics are certified for their achievements. This occurs at present primarily through membership of the ILT, and in many institutions by way of a certificate indicating the completion of a probationary period. This type of assessment takes into account a variety of components such as written assessments, project work, peer observation and student evaluations of teaching and learning. In such cases judgements are made and judgemental assessment or summative assessment occurs, thus producing a decision for the record. Such a decision reflects whether or not the individual has reached the required standard.

Formative and summative assessment can and often do get confused in practice. The essence of formative assessment is that it provides feedback to academics during the learning and developmental period; it should provide the type of information that gives academics the opportunity to improve and learn from their feedback.

In both, formative and summative assessment judgements are made, the difference being that formative assessment directly serves the needs of the academic, while summative assessment primarily serves the needs of the external community, ie those of the probation board or the accreditation purposes of the ILT.

The role of assessment

From the above description it has been possible to establish the purposes of assessment. It is now necessary to consider the role of assessment and how that fits within the professional development framework of an academic. The central argument put forward here is that assessment has two definitive roles, that of accountability from an institutional perspective and that of development and enhanced learning opportunities from the individual's perspective.

Before assessing any phenomenon it is necessary to know what it is for. In Chapter 3, a description was given of the nature of learning, both personal and professional, for the academic. These approaches can and should impact on the nature of assessment for the individual concerned. Thus, the central premise here is that any assessment conducted should assist the academic to learn and provide feedback that encourages reflection on both a personal and professional level. In Chapter 3 learning is defined essentially as changes in knowledge, understanding, skills and attitudes brought about by experience and reflection upon that experience, whether that experience is structured or not. If learning requires such changes, then assessment must also be about those changes.

Assessment within professional development needs to reflect the specific processes of learning. However, at present it appears that process-orientated professional development programmes are still being assessed through traditional assessment strategies, which tend to examine what participants have learnt rather than whether they can apply, analyse and critically reflect on what they have learnt. Thus assessment needs to be an integral part of the development process and focus on learning.

The role of assessment for the individual

The argument for the role of assessment for the individual has often been associated with assessment's contribution to motivation through the recognition of achievement. Research has shown that the way individuals learn is directed by both personality and motivation (Wittrock, 1986; Berliner, 1996). This research suggests that learners perceive themselves and the way they account for their learning success and failures as having a strong connection to their motivation and performance. In the professional context new and experienced academics involved in the learning process must be given the opportunity to learn how to frame and reframe the complex and often ambiguous problems they face when trying to interpret and modify their practice and behaviour (Schön, 1988).

Schön distinguishes reflection *in* action, which is akin to immediate decision making, and reflection *on* action, which provides a longer and deeper view. Schön gives a perspective to reflection that helps the discussion surrounding assessment. However, it is difficult to think of assessing reflection in action and on action. A different perspective, such as that put forward by Halton and Smith, is more helpful. They suggest that 'reflection might be defined as deliberate thinking about action with a view to its improvement' (1995: 52).

How can this statement help in terms of assessment of the academic, if reflection is a key and essential aspect of self-development? Academics should be facilitated in this process. Reflection occurs at many levels, but of particular relevance is the level at which academics' reflective experience should be assessed (if at all). Consideration of Kolb (1976,1984) learning cycles provides a useful discussion framework.

Kolb saw the learning process as being composed of a four-stage cycle, as can be seen in Figure 4.2. Immersion in immediate concrete experience is viewed as the basis for observation and reflection. Observations are assimilated into an idea, image or theory from which implications for future action may be derived. These implications, hunches or hypotheses then guide planning and implementation of experimental action to create new experiences (CE), leading to reflection on these experiences (RO), integration of the observations into more abstract conceptual schemes or theories (AC) and use of these theories to guide decision making and experimental action to solve problems (AE), which leads to new concrete experiences.

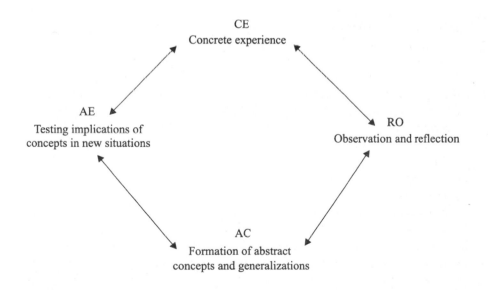

Figure 4.2   Kolb's experiential learning cycle

The useful aspect of the cycle is that it demonstrates that different learning situations foster different skills. An effective environment highlights experiencing of concrete events; a symbolic environment emphasizes abstract conceptualization; a perceptual environment emphasizes observation; and a behavioural environment stresses taking experimental actions. What one needs to develop is an encounter with each element of the cycle. Kolb claimed that individuals' preferred learning styles become more effective the more they reflect the completed cycle.

What this cycle allows us to do is capture aspects of learning experiences that can then point to practical implications, including the desirability of maximizing the opportunity of any experience to support learning and hence develop both personally and professionally. What this theory offers is an explanation of how learning through a particular experience takes place; it does not, however, tell us whether the individual can transfer this learning to other situations. This is where a second set of learning cycles would be needed for the additional learning necessary in the everyday environment for the learning to impact on the individual's job performance. Each set of cycles requires reflection, but the second requires critical reflection at a deeper and more meaningful level.

What is it to be a critical, reflective learner and should we assess such a process if true development and learning are to occur? Surely what is required of academics is to realize and engage with the process, a process that should become second nature in all aspects of their learning and work, whether this be teaching, learning or research.

The assessment procedures as imposed by the ILT and reinforced through institutional programmes fly against the notion of being truly reflexive, a capacity that higher education emphasizes as characteristic of its being. Reflexive capacity on both a personal and professional level is crucial to the development of the academic within the environment of the higher education institution. Barnett states clearly that 'reflection and critical evaluation, therefore, have to contain moments of the creation of imaginary alternatives. Reflexivity has to offer resources for continuing development' (1997: 6).

Critical reflection of this nature is not the territory of students alone; academics themselves are learners and as such need the same resource for continual development. Higher education has the responsibility for providing the climate for criticality for students and academics alike. Critical self-reflection is not just essential but a prerequisite to learning and developing. What is at odds with this essential component of professional development is the assumption that it can be assessed, and in such a way that academics can obtain a seal of approval for developing and achieving a required standard in reflective thinking within the field of teaching, learning and scholarship. Surely what one should be striving for is critical self-reflection that aids development for its own sake, not because it is going to be assessed. Here lies the paradox of the present situation of assessed professional development in higher education.

Assessment in this way is being used for administrative purposes, for example to answer questions such as: are these academics suited to teaching, should they be accredited by the ILT, or should they pass their probationary year? These types of questions should not determine the nature or purpose of professional development. In situations where teaching, learning and scholarship may not be of the quality expected, professional development should be encouraged as a means of learning and developing, creating a situation that engages with and positively promotes critical self-reflection. Professional development should not be seen as an imposition and a type of development that encourages and forces compliance.

Compliance of this nature creates a serious and potentially damaging situation. If compliance is the motivating factor for being assessed favourably, does this then not suggest academics will 'play the game' as a means to an end, ie obtaining recognition for competence in teaching and learning, so that they can then pursue what is believed to be the real reason they came into higher education: research. After all, one of the main arguments in the vast literature related to assessment is that it shows assessment tends to drive individuals' behaviour. If this is the case there is a need to ensure that assessment methods are compatible with the aims of professional development in higher education. It is therefore essential that any assessment schedule needs to reflect the philosophy of reflective practice, as well as integrating the key concepts of professional development. The emphasis must be on the integration of a professional development programme as a whole, rather than superficial assessment of individual cognitive areas. The programme needs to recognize that academics have many areas for development including teaching and learning, and that these areas cannot and should not be separated from academics' disciplines.

If this argument is to hold it is essential to consider now what is being assessed or what it is attempted to assess.

What is being assessed?

It has already been stated that the literature on assessment shows that in higher education there is a relationship between assessment and learning. As professional development has been positioned within a learning framework in Chapters 3 and 6, it becomes essential that we understand what exactly is being (or is going to be) assessed and the implications of that assessment on both academics and their institutions. Figure 4.3 highlights areas of possible assessment

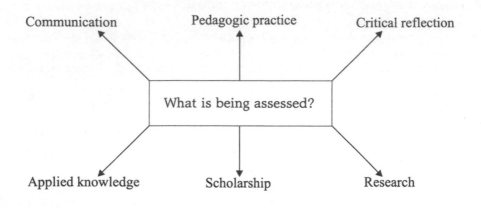

Figure 4.3   What is being assessed?

The argument so far has related to new and experienced academics involved in their disciplines, with teaching, learning and scholarship directly related to that discipline. This suggests that although there are generic qualities and common elements to teaching, learning and scholarship, academics perceive their work primarily as led by their own discipline. Becher summarizes the notion of knowledge and disciplines well: 'It would seem, then, that attitudes, activities and cognitive styles of groups of academics representing a particular discipline are closely bound up with the characteristics and structures of the knowledge domains with which such groups are professionally concerned' (1989: 20).

This being the case, assessment should reflect the above perception, and as such a consideration of professional knowledge and its relationship to professional development is required. Becher's central premise shows us that academics are so closely linked to their disciplines that to detach their own learning and development from them is nonsensical. 'The ways in which particular groups of academics organize their professional lives are innately related to the intellectual tasks on which they are engaged' (1996: 21).

Considering the types of knowledge academics might need as professionals helps the discussion. Eraut's (1994, 1995) work suggests that professional knowledge can be categorized in such a way as to help view development. Eraut (1994) distinguishes between different types of knowledge, how they are acquired and their role in professional action. He suggests three broad areas: propositional knowledge, personal knowledge and process knowledge.

Propositional knowledge contains three subcategories:

1. discipline-based theories and concepts derived from bodies of coherent systematic knowledge;
2. generalizations and practical principles in the applied field of professional action;
3. specified propositions about particular cases, decisions and actions.

Such knowledge may get used in one of four ways: replication, application, interpretation or association. Together they account for aspects of discipline-based knowledge that make up parts of professional knowledge.

The second form of knowledge is described as *personal knowledge*, which is composed of impressions and knowledge acquired through experience. *Process knowledge* is defined as knowing how to conduct the various processes that contribute to the professional action. This can be taken as Ryle's (1944) distinction between 'knowing that' and 'knowing how'. Within Eraut's distinctions of types of knowledge he adds that of *professional knowledge*. This, he suggests, includes acquiring information, skilled behaviour, deliberate processes such as planning and decision making, giving information and metacognitive processes such as control of behaviour. These categories give us an indication of the complexity of the knowledge areas the academic is working with. Candy (1994) adapted and further developed Eraut's three distinctions to produce five areas of skills that professionals require if they are to progress within their given profession. These include:

1. knowledge skills;
2. thinking skills;
3. personal skills;
4. personal attributes;
5. practical skills.

For the purpose of this discussion the knowledge skills and thinking skills form the basis of the argument. This is not to say that personal skills and attributes, and practical skills are not important; they are. However, in terms of assessment the former two aspects are key elements.

Knowledge skills

Let us consider knowledge skills and how these could relate to issues within a given discipline. When referring to teaching this involves what Shulman (1987) calls 'subject-pedagogy' or a 'pedagogy of substance'. 'It involves mastery of that variety of ways (demonstrated by expert teachers) by which the particular concepts of a field are translated (transformed) into terms accessible to and understandable by students at their particular stages of development' (Edgerton, Hutchings and Quinlan, 1991: 2). Such knowledge is at the heart of a scholarship of teaching (see Chapter 6). It is a type of knowledge that is integrally related to the deep knowledge of a discipline, and demands a clearly articulated notion of what constitutes knowledge within the given discipline. Taylor provides us with a description of knowledge-based information that may help in identifying areas for assessment. The analysis put forward considers content (substantive knowledge), problem solving (thinking and reasoning strategies), epistemic norms and values, and modes of inquiry and criticism (1993: 69–70).

Within Taylor's description there is an implicit notion that learning occurs. The knowledge base provided by him fits well with Ryle's 'knowing that' and knowing how' concept. These two aspects can be recategorized into two elements, conceptual knowledge and procedural knowledge: whereas procedures provide the means to secure goals and sub-goals, concepts provide a conceptual basis to guide the goal-directed activity of problem solving (thinking and acting), as well as goals for performance.

Problem solving is an important element as it is central to securing cognitive development. Both conceptual and procedural knowledge are used in everyday practice to organize activities and secure workplace goals. Procedural knowledge secures goals that concepts provide. An example here is that of a mathematician wishing to introduce the concepts related to higher order calculus. Before this occurs he or she must be aware of the procedures involved within the concepts, as well as the variety of procedures that may be used to teach the concepts. This requires an understanding of both the discipline-based knowledge and what Shulman calls the subject-pedagogy.

Conceptual knowledge is differentiated by levels of complexity or depth (Evans, 1991; Greeno, 1989). These levels range from simple factual knowledge through to more complex levels of conceptual knowledge. The importance here to development is that the richer the association and interconnectedness of the conceptual knowledge, the more likely individuals are to transfer their conceptual knowledge. This makes conceptual knowledge significant, as it permits the formulation of goals and assists with the deployment of procedures to secure workplace performance. This type of knowledge and thinking in conjunction with good procedural knowledge allows the experienced and expert academic to analyse problems and offer more effective solutions than novice or inexperienced academics achieve.

Professional development that encourages experienced and inexperienced academics to work together can bridge the gap between the use of procedural knowledge and conceptual knowledge. It is at this juncture that the development of reflective skills is needed. If academics are to translate their discipline-based knowledge into effective pedagogy two things need to happen. First, they must learn the techniques, rules and guidelines of the different forms of inquiry within their discipline; different elements call for different skills. Second, they must learn about themselves, and what it means to be part of the different elements of their discipline. They must attend not only to the knowledge and skills of chemistry, law or history, but also to themselves as future chemists, lawyers or historians within the academic community and the world at large. They must address what it means to have 'competence' in both these areas. Essential to the above is the understanding of what it means to be reflective.

Reflective skills (thinking skills)

The concept of 'reflection', reflective practice and critical reflective learning has been and continues to be an important aspect of professional development. Research has shown (Boud, Keogh and Walker, 1985; Kolb, 1984; Burnard, 1995) that reflection on experience can be thought of as a vehicle through which learning occurs. Hence reflecting directly on professional practice should be a core element of the academic's work. Mezirow reminds us that 'reflection is generally used as a synonym for higher order mental processes. However, it demands more than drawing on what one already knows in order to act, it requires critical thinking aimed at examining and justifying one's beliefs' (1992: 5). This suggests that if academics are to develop their practice, a process including both personal and professional growth, then critical reflection on practice will be central to the learning. Here development is taken as moving beyond the acquisition of new knowledge and understanding, into questioning existing assumptions, values and perspectives.

Dewey's definition of reflection is useful here to take the discussion forward. He considers reflection as 'active persistent and careful consideration of any belief or supposed form of knowledge in the light of the grounds that support it and further conclusion to which it tends' (1933: 9). What Dewey is referring to here is the need for individuals to learn to think, by being able to 'discriminate between beliefs that rest upon tested evidence and those that do not' (p 97). This process can be summarized as follows. When individuals think, they delay action until they:

- understand the situation thoroughly;
- know the goals they want to reach;
- have considered as many options as possible for reaching that goal;
- have assessed the options they have;
- have made a plan before taking action.

Dewey's view is that being able to discriminate between those things that are beliefs and those things that are based on evidence is a 'critical factor… in all reflective or distinctively intellectual thinking' (1933: 11). This type of reflection is closely linked to Mezirow's notion of critical self-reflection, and key to changing and developing the individual. Essential to all these definitions of reflection is the individual as the key participant, who understands what it is to reflect and be involved in the reflective process.

If reflective learning is to impact on the quality of teaching, learning and scholarship, we as an academic community need to be clear as to the aims and purposes of the process we are being asked to engage in, especially in relation to the demands of the ILT. Clearly, if reflection is to be part of an overall assessment strategy it must take account of generic and discipline-based knowledge and skills. Assessing the process of reflection, reflective dialogue and critical reflective learning needs to be addressed differently if it is to be an effective tool for development within the academic community. Critical reflection is central to the process of transformative learning and change. But, not all critical reflection leads to transformation and change; we can question and inquire without having to change things. For transformative change to occur the process of reflection has to involve and lead to some fundamental change in perspective and consequent action.

Personal reflection, often evidenced in the form of a self-report or reflective narrative, is the only evidence that may be produced to show change, development and learning. Assessment of such evidence needs to place value on self-reports and critical narrative, but at the same time must ensure reliability, coherence and clear criteria for the assessment.

At present the nature of reflection and reflective learning as required for accreditation to the ILT requires assessment of the summative or inspectorial kind. This tends to go against the true nature of critical reflective learning. Brockbank and McGill suggest that looking at the Latin origins of the term 'assessment', 'to sit beside', allows us to consider the meaning and values being promoted in critical reflective learning as being collaborative rather than inspectorial (1998: 6). If this is the case we need to ask the questions: how is the assessment process addressing the issue of evidence related to critical reflective learning, from both a generic and discipline perspective? How is the reflective learning process being assessed?

At the very least the academic being assessed should know and understand what is required for and through the assessment process. An assessment strategy that uses the process of critical reflective learning must clearly demonstrate how and what is to be assessed in terms of outcome and process. The following should be transparent (modified from Brockbank and McGill, 1998: 102):

● the way critical reflective learning in terms of outcomes within a discipline is identified;

- the way that reflective dialogue has taken place and been ascertained (with peers and colleagues);
- the way evidence of the learner's participation in the dialogue is established;
- the way evidence of a developmental process over time, regardless of the start or end-point, is identified;
- the way evidence of the review system is used, which should enable an understanding of the learning process that has taken place, and should be recorded.

If evidence of reflective learning is used constructively it should demonstrate Mezirow's three types of reflection that lead to transformation and change. These are content reflection, process reflection and premise reflection. The nature of this evidence might be found in:

- learning review;
- review records;
- reflective commentary or narrative;
- reviewer and peer reports.

What constitutes the three types of reflection suggested?

Content reflection

Content reflection produces the type of reflection advocated by Dewey (1933). It allows individuals to reflect on the content or description of a problem, ie it facilitates individuals to 'learn how to think, and discriminate between beliefs that rest upon tested evidence and those that do not'. For example, if academics have a problem with integrating their research into their teaching, they might look for indicators of appropriate points within the module or curriculum to introduce the research and link them closely with effective teaching strategies. If they then notice that the research is being better understood and applied successfully by the students, the academics might then wish to develop the strategies further to incorporate more research into their teaching. This type of reflection can help academics perceive their work within the context of their discipline, and change their pedagogic practice through concentrating their reflection on their research and scholarship.

Figure 4.4 shows the nature of possible steps taken to achieve change. Within each step identified in the figure, evidence relating to reflection, planning, research and teaching can be documented and recorded.

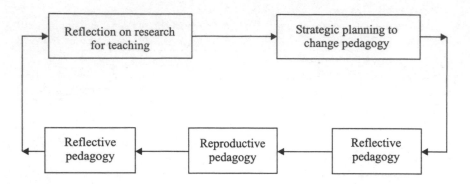

Figure 4.4 Examples of content reflection

Process reflection

This stage of reflection relates to thinking about the strategies pursued to solve the identified problem, rather than the content of the problem itself. Here academics might ask whether or not the routes chosen to find indicators for integrating research into their teaching were adequate. The questions they should be attempting to answer are:

- Are the indicators relevant?
- Are the indicators dependable?
- Are the indicators transferable to other situations?
- Are the indicators helpful to solving the problem?

Figure 4.5 shows how the reflective process incorporates process reflection in the original example, allowing individuals to consider how to think about the original problem and to establish how far they have gone in solving it.

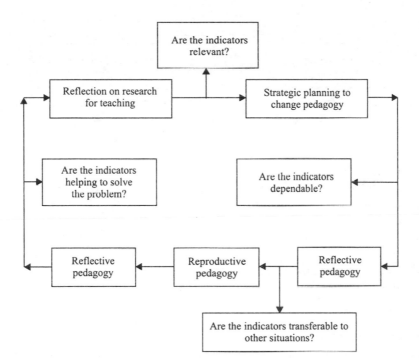

Figure 4.5   Incorporating process reflection

Premise reflection

Within the context of teaching, learning and scholarship this might well be the most important aspect of reflection. It assists in asking the question: what is the relevance of the problem itself? In our example, the question would relate to relevance of trying to integrate recent research into teaching. The academic might wish to approach this issue by asking the following questions:

- Is integrating my research into my teaching my concern and responsibility?
- Should my research be integrated into my teaching?
- Is the integration of new research findings a valid approach to teaching?
- Are my research findings of any relevance to my teaching?

These questions are crucial for academics to understand and be aware of. Premise reflection allows individuals to examine the assumptions under which their beliefs and values underline the problem being addressed.

In essence critical reflection by individuals should allow them to see the expectations they have of themselves, their students and their role in an academic community. If this is the case reflective academics can begin to question and examine these assumptions and become free to choose to revise them if they are found to be distorted, unreliable or invalid.

Perceiving academics as critically reflective practitioners and learners casts doubts on the merits of attempting to assess reflection as a means of enhancing the quality of teaching and learning. The premise of this statement lies in the fact that creating critical reflective academics is not a matter of improving techniques, but rather a process of engaging academics in understanding why they do what they do. If academics truly engage in reflective practice, a consequence of this action will be a 'real change' in practice based on articulating the assumptions underlying it, realizing the consequences of those assumptions, critically questioning the assumptions and, as Barnett says, 'imaging alternatives' to current perspectives and practices.

The nature of accreditation at present does not appear to reflect or even demand this depth of reflection, nor has it clear criteria for assessment. Thus it is possible to argue that the way academics are asked to engage in the reflective process at present could do the academic community a disservice. The process does not allow academics to become truly reflective in the way previously described, as such higher-order thinking skills are not required to be demonstrated in the way suggested by Mezirow.

Assessment and competence

The above section started with the question: what is being assessed? The main argument showed that the nature of the assessment academics are now involved in with respect to the ILT is not conducive to true reflection. If this is the case, what type of assessment model is it moving towards?

It would appear that competence in teaching and learning is high on the agenda of the ILT. Enhancing the quality of teaching and learning in higher education is laudable and indeed necessary, but is the notion of competence a useful way forward within professional development? Competence can mean a variety of things to a variety of people, as do the implications of competency models of development. One meaning of competence, which could be useful, is that it is regarded as a stage on the way to proficiency and expertise. A competent professional is no longer a novice or a beginner and can be trusted with a degree of responsibility in those areas within the range of his or her competence, but has not yet become proficient or expert (Eraut, 1994: 215).

This is different from a competency-based model, which is underpinned by a binary system of assessment, in which judgements are restricted to whether the individual is competent or not. This type of assessment is inappropriate to most areas of professional knowledge (Eraut, 1994: 216). Interestingly this system continues to exist and is rarely challenged. At present all initial teacher education is based on such a model, and increasingly Health Service education is moving rapidly in this direction. This is reflected in the new nursing, midwifery and health visiting standards (UKCC, 2000). Is it possible that a competency system could dominate the training and development of new and existing lecturers in higher education? Certainly the generic formulation of knowledge and skills expected to be demonstrated for membership to the ILT shows more than embryonic elements of such a binary system of assessment. A competency-based system would be contrary to the development of the diverse role of the academic. The implication here is not that we do not require the quality of teaching and learning in higher education to be raised, but that a competency model of assessment that could be continually scrutinized and possibly inspected does not sit well with the notion of academic freedom and the role of facilitating learning. It might satisfy the appetite of those who feel accountability in teaching and learning must be assessable against a baseline competence, but it won't necessarily enhance the quality of teaching and learning in higher education.

If competency-based assessment is allowed to develop, the notion of reflection and transformative learning in its truest sense, a sense in which we would want academics to develop, will not only be elusive to the academic community, but will possibly disappear. Ultimately will we classify lecturers as good, bad, etc, or even give them ratings synonymous with RAE ratings? Could this be the future assessment of teaching and learning in higher education? One could envisage research ratings and teaching ratings based on individual competence. This is theoretically possible, but destructive to the concept of lifelong learning and learning within an academic community.

Although we are not at present in a formalized competency-based system, it is difficult to see where further learning and progressive learning rest in the model we have. It is a model that is increasingly becoming prescriptive and more assessable. Will gaining entry into the ILT actually make a difference? A certificate or, in the case of the ILT, acceptance as a member may actually signify a critical change in the status of the academic and mark a decline in the amount of time he or she then gives formally to professional learning, especially learning that relates to pedagogic issues. However, what professional development in higher education should be aiming for is not a disjointed learning and developmental process, but a progressive process that encourages and acknowledges continuity and progression in both personal and professional learning.

The academic community should be looking to develop a coherent system of learning and development for academics, at whatever stage in their career, which reflects the diversity of roles they are engaged in and ensures that the whole learn-ing/development process is acknowledged and rewarded.

Monitoring development: the case of continuity and progression

Institutions should be looking to develop systems that are coherent, progressive and allow for points of transition in the academic career. Professional development is crucial at points of transition. Figure 4.6 shows a simple linear progressive route of development within higher education. It is accepted here that alternatives to this linear path occur. However, generally the linearity is observed. What is important here to development are the points of transition, because here the community makes judgements and assessments about individuals, often requiring new things from academics before transfer to the next stage is endorsed, eg lecturer to senior lecturer. Let us consider and trace the career path of new young academics.

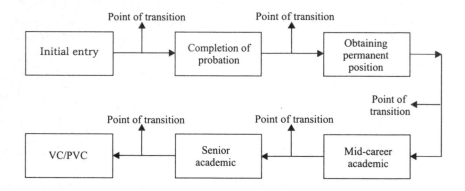

Figure 4.6   Progression and continuity through transition points

Initial entry to the academy

Assessment first occurs before individuals are appointed, eg are they academically qualified in their given discipline to fulfil their role as 'lecturer' (whatever that role may constitute)? On taking up their position, more often than not new academics are asked to:

- teach;
- develop course modules;
- assess students' work;
- become personal tutors;
- write research bids;
- engage with research;
- publish papers;
- give seminars;
- attend conferences.

Ask the question: what experience do these young, highly motivated, intelligent individuals have of all these expectations, and how does the present system or any future system aim to help them? Clearly, the assessment made of them to obtain the position was that they could and would perform these tasks adequately. The first point of transition and area for development is creating a learning environment that encourages new academics to grow and become 'competent' in the demands and expectations made of them. At this stage assessment should be formative and developmental with the following aims:

- to foster and ensure a learning environment that allows for the fundamental competencies to be gained;
- to allow individuals the opportunity to develop beyond this through making alternative learning experiences occur both educationally and in the workplace;
- to be responsive and sympathetic to the qualities and preferences of individual learners.

Judgements made should encourage the type of learning and reflection that academics need to foster in order to continue learning from their learning. This progression needs to be perceived at an early stage as crucial to both personal and professional development.

At the end of this period judgements and assessments are once again made as to whether probation has been successfully completed. This period includes entry into the ILT, which demonstrates 'competence' to teach. If assessed positively, academics transfer and enter a new phase in their career path and face another point of transition. They are no longer new and inexperienced, but at the same time they are not considered experienced enough to take major responsibilities. Individuals, as they transfer from being probationers to tenured members of staff, need support. How is this transition managed in terms of professional development? How is 'transfer' recognized?

The above questions need to be asked at each point in the continuum of development. This is particularly so in higher education where increasingly skills such as financial management, organizational change, and interaction at national and international policy level are expected, as well as the establishment of excellent teaching/learning environments within a continually changing technological world. Academics do not automatically possess all of these skills, yet increasingly they are being assessed on and judged by their performance within the areas. Professional development has to encompass these elements for individual academics from both the personal and professional dimension. For a community of professional learners who have to meet the demands of constant and continual change, their progress along a career pathway has to be given more attention, particularly at the points of transition and transfer.

Each transitional point requires:

- extending competence over a wider range of situations, context demands and knowledge base;
- developing increased autonomy and independence, with less reliance on support and advice;
- developing the skills to make certain tasks and jobs routine;
- learning and developing the skills to deal with increased workloads, and external and internal demands;
- developing the knowledge base and skills that will assist competence in further and future roles;
- developing the ability to extend professional capability and experience;
- developing a reflexive approach to personal learning as a means to improving one's quality of work.

The above points adapted from Eraut (1994) need to be considered as a continuum of development and learning process. The elements should be coherent, allowing progression and continuity in academic learning. They do not have to be synonymous with professional development records that will be assessed for pre- or post-qualification, as is presently being suggested by the ILT. The process needs to reflect the goals and values of higher education, those of creative, reflexive, autonomous learners, who are professionally accountable.

How can assessment be part of professional accountability?

It can be argued that the academy and those within it do require autonomy in the exercise of expertise – but autonomy needs to be counterbalanced by a clear structure of public accountability. The question for higher education institutions is whether their structures of accountability with respect to teaching, learning and professional development are sufficiently clear and strong. Has it been that higher education's inability to assure the public and increasingly now its stakeholders – students who pay fees – of uniform and effective performance evaluation suggests that a key element of professionalism may indeed be missing? For professionalism means that service to a clientele and the good of that clientele are paramount, and regularly reviewed. Is it because the standing of higher education on these matters has not been assured that we now have a system and possible future systems that attempt to enforce assurance through a variety of assessment processes?

Higher education must and possibly does accept the notion of accountability, particularly in its professional role. It is time that higher education looked critically at itself and learnt from what it often cites as important to others, that of being a critically reflective learning community. Barnett discusses this notion in *The Limits of Competence* when talking about the relationship of society and higher education:

> The modern state will exert its claims on higher education both operationally and – even more significantly – in its inner forms of life. What counts as knowledge and education will be changed, if the state has an unchallenged time of it. In some way those changes will be beneficial: internal definitions of knowledge and education may be widened. But in other ways, those changes may lead to narrowing of human consciousness. Understanding is replaced by competence, insight is replaced by effectiveness, and rigour of interactive argument is replaced by communication skills.
>
> (Barnett, 1994: 37)

The question is whether higher education will be able to reflect self-critically on its position in terms of professional development, and thus create and allow for a genuine learning community to evolve. Or must its changes be led by external bodies, with imposed development strategies, regulated levels of competence and an assessment process that does not reflect the values and goals of a higher education learning community?

5

A new professionalism for higher education?

Jon Nixon

Introduction

In Chapter 2 the demands and functions of the ILT were introduced and discussed, highlighting some of the issues related to the professional and the role of professional bodies. This chapter explores and extends the ways in which academic staff working within the context of higher education might be seen as professionals with a shared set of values and expectations. It argues that the changing conditions of higher education have made it extremely difficult to speak of academic workers as a unified 'profession'. Moreover, the stratification of higher education has led to increased and deepening divisions of labour within which academic workers have become increasingly isolated, while also becoming increasingly accountable. The only way out of this impasse, it is argued, is for academics to redefine their professionalism in terms of their underlying commitments and purposes. That task of redefinition is discussed in terms of a distinction between two competing notions of 'academic freedom': the traditional notion of 'academic freedom' as *freedom for academics* and an emergent notion of 'academic freedom' as *freedom for others*.

It is with reference to that emergent notion that this chapter speculates upon the possibility of a new professionalism for higher education, while recognizing that a new professionalism of this kind would be deeply at odds with the prevailing managerialism of higher education as manifest in its quality control mechanisms, accountability procedures and planned systems of professional accreditation. Within the UK, the Dearing-inspired Institute for Learning and Teaching in Higher Education is currently establishing a system of professional accreditation that is wrong-headed both in its restrictive emphasis on threshold competencies and in its assumption that there is a single 'right' way to conceptualize teaching. The ILT has adopted a model of professional development that places uniformity and comparability of outcome above quality and creativity of process. Such a model may identify a minimal checklist of professional requirements. It will certainly provide a useful 'policing' instrument. However, it has no potential as a framework within which teachers in higher education can learn, produce ideas, enhance their practice and engage more fully with their various 'users'. If the intention is to ensure that academic staff are accountable for reflecting on and improving their teaching and for judging the adequacy of what they do, then it is essential that whatever approach is adopted should encourage them not only to describe what they do but also to explain and justify, in thoughtful and productive ways, *why they do what they do*.

What is needed in respect of professional development in higher education is not a new apparatus of control and accreditation, but a reformulation of academic practice with a view to generating new forms of participation in and access to the intrinsic goods of learning. This chapter does not provide a technology of professional development such as is currently being developed under the auspices of the ILT. What it does do is advocate a renewed sense of purposefulness in respect of professional development within higher education and specify some of the implications of approaching professional development in this way. A key assumption underlying the argument is that professional development is necessarily and primarily a matter of addressing issues of principle and value in one's own teaching and learning practices.

The changing conditions of higher education

Higher education is undergoing a series of complex overlapping changes, which are profoundly affecting its organizational structures, traditional practices and the way in which its institutions and those who work within them are viewed by the public. The challenge it faces must be understood historically in terms of: the dramatic expansion in student numbers over the last 30 years together with a steady reduction in resources; consequent changes in curriculum, teaching and assessment; changes in the conditions of academic work; and changing structures of accountability and professional accreditation.

The changing student body

The Robbins Report (1963) looked forward to a modest increase in student numbers within a system not fundamentally different from the previous one of highly restricted access. From 1963 to 1990, however, the expansion of higher education far exceeded these expectations: in 1962 the total number of full-time students in the higher education system was 216,000; by 1989/90, including home and overseas students, part-timers in universities, the Open University, the then polytechnics and other colleges offering advanced courses, it was 1,086,300 (Halsey, 1992a). By 1995/96 the total number of higher education students in the UK had risen to between 1.6 and 1.8 million with the number of universities almost quadrupling in the period 1960–90 (Watson and Taylor, 1998: 4, 11).

Moreover, this expansion brought with it a much less homogeneous student population. Whilst children of working-class families and members of some minority ethnic groups continued to be under-represented, women and part-time students now made up a greater proportion of the total (with the growth in participation by women being a particular feature of the new universities and of part-time courses). The age profile was also changing: 'Between 1981 and 1991 the number of mature first year students on undergraduate courses almost tripled, from 26,000 to over 70,000, such that nearly one in three entrants were aged 21 and over by the end of this period' (Parry, 1995: 110). Overall the pattern of student entry was such that, by 1990, more mature students entered higher education in Great Britain than young students, with 80 per cent of all mature students located in the new universities (National Commission on Education, 1993: 293). The traditional image of transition at 18-plus from school or college to university had become, for many institutions, an anachronism.

Changes in curriculum, teaching and assessment

These changes in the student population have led to diversification of course content and structure and to an increased emphasis on differentiating the educational needs of students, with modularization and credit accumulation now established as important organizational elements in almost all universities. The shift is away 'from an early notion of access based on defined routes and discrete courses to one more centrally concerned with the "accessibility" of institutions and the suitability and flexibility of their curricula for a diverse student audience' (Parry, 1995: 125). Entwistle (1992) has summarized some of the main elements of that shift in terms of the kinds of teaching methods currently being practised within the context of higher education: lectures; resource-based learning, open learning and distance education; instructional technology and computer-based learning; discussion classes and simulations; peer-teaching and co-operative project work; and supervised work experience and learning contracts. What is important about these current practices, argues Entwistle, is not just the variety of methods adopted, but the emphasis placed upon 'self-regulated learning' and upon students becoming increasingly aware of their own studying and thinking processes, an emphasis that is also evident in the shift towards 'formative' assessment procedures including self- and peer-assessment and the development of 'learner agreements' (Opacic, 1994).

Changing conditions of academic work

Alongside the changing patterns of student intake and of curriculum and pedagogy are immense changes in the staffing structures of higher education. An OECD study of institutional management in higher education argues that the cohesion afforded by traditional structures 'is likely to be eroded as status and other differentials increase, especially between staff with permanent appointments and those in temporary or part-time contracts'. The report goes on to argue that 'it is no longer sensible to speak of a single academic profession' and that 'a caste distinction is emerging between "have" and "have-not" groups'. The latter constitute 'an underclass... with limited prospects for advancement or employment stability'. At the same time increased differentials and tensions are apparent among what the report calls 'top-level academics' who are under pressure to produce high-profile research and to develop and market new and appealing courses (Kogan, Moses and El-Khawas, 1994: 62–63).

So, whilst the economic power of some senior academics has been increased by the current climate of competition, others feel deprived of the significance to which they think their academic status should entitle them: 'they are less secure in their position within their own institution, and subject to more public criticism... They work at a pace dictated by external pressures' (Wright, 1997: 6–7). The result is that different and often incompatible structures are emerging with different groups occupied on different tasks and often pursuing different interests. Meanwhile, much of the day-to-day work of teaching and research in universities is sustained by 'a growing army of insecurely employed contract staff who now make up to a third of all academic employees' (Ainley, 1994: 32). This process might best be described as one of Balkanization, although (as Ryan, 1999, points out) it is also yet another instance of UK policy in pursuit of 'the American way'. (Martin, 1999 and Smyth, 1995 provide useful points of international comparison with regard to the changing conditions of academic labour.)

The changing structures of accountability and accreditation

Attempts by the ILT to corral academic professionalism within the parameters of outcome statements and competence thresholds are just another instance of the increasingly accountability-driven, outcomes-orientated, quality-control culture of higher education. The impact of this culture on individuals and on relationships is considered by many academic workers to be deeply damaging, as the following heartfelt statement suggests:

> What is not possible without irreparable damage to the relationships at stake in a good university education... is the general application of bureaucratic procedures that purport to shape and measure how all the individuals concerned teach and engage in the pursuit of knowledge. Yet it is a model of this kind that inspires the stream of 'assessment' procedures with which universities are now afflicted, all of which add to the 'red tape' cutting in on time available for the real work of academics. It no longer matters how well an academic teaches and whether he or she sometimes inspires their pupils; it is far more important that they have produced plans of their courses, bibliographies, outlines of this, that and the other, in short all the paraphernalia of futile bureaucratization, required for assessors who come from on high like emissaries from Kafka's castle.
>
> (Johnson, 1994: 379)

The chief executive of the Quality Assurance Agency for Higher Education has recently argued that 'professionalism' is a notion more appropriately ascribed to institutions than to individuals and that professionalism therefore should be judged, in part, by the professional infrastructures of the institutions, which support particular professional practices (see Randall, 2000). However, what is at stake in any discussion of professionalism is the complex working out of values at the level not only of organizational structure but of individual and group practice. Practices rely upon the continuity and sustainability that institutions provide, but have their own intrinsic goods to which professionalism owes its ultimate allegiance. What the changing structures of accountability fail to recognize is that these intrinsic goods do not inevitably square with the extrinsic goals and targets of the institution and that, when push comes to shove, practitioners must, in the interests of their own professionalism, back the values implicit in practice.

A crisis of professional identity

A consequence of the changing conditions outlined above is that the occupation of university teacher no longer automatically carries the assumption of autonomy and status. Since autonomy and status have been defining characteristics of occupations that lay claim to being professions, these changes have occasioned a serious debate as to what kind of occupational group, or groups, university teachers now constitute, and have consequently increased many of the tensions inherent in the role of the university teacher. Key questions in the debate concern the extent to which university teachers now constitute: a profession divided against itself; a set of occupations so diverse in their practices that the term 'professional' may no longer be applicable in all or even most cases; a new proletariat with very little opportunity, and even less encouragement, to exercise independent judgement and self-regulation; or a new professional grouping based on alternative values and aspirations.

A divided profession?

The role of university teacher, as Piper has argued, is Janus-faced: 'academics look to their occupation for their identity as teachers, but outside for their identity as subject specialists' (1994: 6). This dual professional identity, which is particularly relevant to those in a professional training role, is becoming increasingly difficult to sustain, both at the level of professional practice and at the level of organizational structure. The changing student intake has placed an emphasis on the need for pedagogical and curriculum change and, consequently, on the professional identity of the university teacher *as teacher*, capable of developing and marketing innovative programmes. At the same time, however, the changing conditions of academic work have placed a premium on the professional identity of the university teacher *as researcher*, capable of attracting external funds within an increasingly competitive research culture.

The system requires of university lecturers an increased investment not only in their own institutions, but in the professional and business communities and the various networks and structures that comprise their particular fields and subject specialisms. Career mobility, moreover, depends increasingly on the individual's reputation and influence outside his or her own institution: 'Spending time with colleagues does not generate research grants and seldom results in publications. Nor does it advance disciplinary knowledge. The incentives to generate and participate in an intellectual life on a university campus are small in comparison to the incentives to engage in an intellectual life off campus' (Steneck, 1994: 19). Increasingly, the pull is outward and upward.

A plurality of occupations?

The stratification of the higher education sector has led to a greater degree of institutional specialization and to sharper divisions of labour within the academic workplace: 'the gulf is widening between a small number of affluent and highly selective institutions where competition for admission is fierce and mostly privilege the wealthy – and hard-pressed public and private institutions' (Gamson, 1998: 109). As a result of this increased stratification, the professional identity of university teachers is being redefined: 'through diversification, several categories of academic workers have been created, each having distinct terms and conditions of employment, including salary scales, benefits, career chances, duties and prerogatives in university governance' (Newson and Buchbinder, 1988: 25). Within the UK these categories, and the differentials between them, are being reinforced through the introduction of teaching-only contracts, the development of specialist research centres and graduate schools within existing institutions, differentiated pay scales, independently negotiated pay settlements for senior academics and an increasing reliance on research contract staff. The academic workforce, in other words, now includes a plurality of occupational groups divided from one another by task, influence and seniority within the institution. In so far as it can be seen as a single professional grouping, it is becoming 'an increasingly part-time profession', 'an increasingly managed profession' and 'an increasingly capitalistic profession, globally' (Rhoades and Slaughter, 1998: 34–35).

The recent emphasis within curriculum design on modular programmes of work and associated systems of assessment has reinforced these divisions through the creation of a 'middle management' tier of course leaders or what Winter calls 'academic managers': 'Responsibility for the overall coherence and progression of students' education is assumed not by the staff who teach individual modules but by the academic managers who design the modular system and by the academic counsellors who guide student choice of modules' (1995: 134). This diversification of the academic workforce is accompanied, both within the UK and elsewhere, by stratification of the student body: 'research-focused graduate students and full-time professors are in a preferred status while teaching-oriented part-timers and classroom-oriented graduates are in a secondary status' (Buchbinder and Rajagopal, 1995: 70).

A new proletariat?

Halsey argues that the fragmentation of the academic workplace is one of a number of material and ideological conditions that, taken together, are transforming university teachers into a new proletariat whose relative class and status advantages are being significantly eroded:

Managerialism gradually comes to dominate collegiate cooperation in the organization of both teaching and research. Explicit vocationalism displaces implicit vocational preparation, as degree courses are adapted to the changing division of labour in the graduate market. Research endeavours are increasingly applied to the requirements of government or industrial demands. The don becomes increasingly a salaried or even a piece-work labourer in the service of an expanding middle class of administrators and technologists.

(Halsey, 1992b: 13)

While no one would disagree that university teachers are in a very different position to, say, craft workers in the 19th-century textile industry, Halsey and others argue that both groups share a lack of 'ideological' control over their work: 'Through their command of discrete expertise, academics can still largely influence the processes of both their research and teaching, but the raw material (students or problems to be investigated) is increasingly determined by the combined influences of the state, institutional managers and the market' (Miller, 1995: 56). These combined influences help create a climate that accords with what Dummett (1994: 1269) has discussed in terms of the 'principles' of insecurity, competition and surveillance:

that each task must be done at the least possible cost; that people work effectively only if they know their jobs are insecure, and if they are lured by increases of salary or of status to be obtained in competition with their colleagues; and that no institution can be trusted to evaluate its own or its employees' efficiency, which must be estimated by having each employee assessed by other employees or by the 'customers', by 'objective' performance indicators or, best of all, by the reports of external inspectors.

A new professionalism?

There is, however, another way of addressing this crisis of professional identity. Nixon *et al* (1997) argue that, within the new management of education, there are indications of an 'emergent' professionalism distinguishable from both the 'residual' and 'dominant' versions of professionalism that are more readily identifiable. Nixon and Ranson (1997) characterize this 'emergent' professionalism in terms of new forms of agreement-making that seek to reinforce the primacy of the relation between professionals and their publics and the need to ground that relation in an ongoing dialogue regarding the ends and purposes of learning. The terms and conditions of that dialogue, it is argued, make for 'learning professions': occupational groups whose sense of professional identity is derived from their capacity to listen to, learn from and move forward with the communities they serve. Nixon (1996, 1997) outlines some of the implications of this outlook for those working within higher education.

This perspective does not seek to deny the fragmentation and alienation of the academic workforce. But it does square up to these problems in a different kind of way. It sees professionalism neither as a benign buffer between the public and the state nor as an oligarchic tendency whereby corporate power serves to increase a particular occupation's leverage. It sees professionalism as the *capacity* of an occupational group to be extrovert, generous and knowledgeable in its relations with professional colleagues, other professional groups and 'the public'. It defines professionalism, therefore, not in terms of status and self-regulation, but in terms of values and practices. Why I do what I do is of the utmost significance, as are the deliberative processes whereby I address that 'why'. Without this emphasis on the moral purposefulness of practice there would be no claim to professionalism.

Shifting the moral bases

Traditionally, that sense of moral purposefulness has turned on the notion of academic freedom as *freedom for academics*: their freedom to speak their own minds, to teach in accordance with their own interests and to develop those interests according to their own research agenda. Even staunch defendants of academic freedom now question its relevance and acknowledge its vulnerability: 'academic freedom is not a strong beacon that illuminates the entire university. It is rather a wavering flame of recent historical development' (Hamilton, 1998: 343). This is all for the best. It is good that academic freedom be seen for what it always was: an attempt to protect the interests of a particular occupational group. Of course, that group espouses and, at best, practises important values – intellectual honesty, scholastic rigour, self-examination, respect for divergent views, etc – without which any democratic society would be greatly impoverished. But the version of professionalism to which the notion of academic freedom has sought to lend credibility remains inward-looking and self-referential. Academic freedom is, ultimately, freedom for the academic.

A common critical response to this version of academic freedom is that it is rapidly becoming obsolete. Academic freedom, Menand argues (1996), has depended crucially upon the autonomy and integrity of the disciplines. 'For it is the departments, and the disciplines to which they belong, that constitute the spaces in which rival scholarly and pedagogical positions are negotiated. Academic freedom not only protects sociology professors from the interface of trustees and public officials in the exercise of their jobs as teachers and scholars; it protects them from physics professors as well' (Menand, 1996: 17).

With what Menand calls 'the meltdown of disciplinary boundaries' (p 18), these protective 'spaces' are no longer available. The traditional sense of 'belonging' to a disciplinary tradition is being replaced by a sense of 'belonging' to an institution. The significance of 'the meltdown', insists Menand, is 'not epistemological or political. It is, much more banally, administrative. Universities differ' (p 17). Increasingly, it is these institutional differences, rather than the disciplinary traditions that provide a space for academic freedom, to which academics look for their sense of 'belonging'. Moreover, the institutional conditions of academic work are so tightly hedged in by reward and accountability systems that academic freedom, although still evoked, is in practice increasingly difficult to exercise. A freedom that rebounds negatively upon those who try to exercise it is not particularly liberating. It may be a consolation under these circumstances for academics to tell themselves that they 'enjoy' academic freedom. In practice, however, that enjoyment is becoming increasingly illusory. 'In such an environment,' argues Barnett (1997: 53), 'academic freedom is not taken away; rather, the opportunities for its realization are reduced.' (As Barnett, 2000: 173–74, also points out, it is not insignificant that while the Robbins Report of 1963 devotes an entire chapter to the subject of 'academic freedom and its scope', the Dearing Report of 1997 considers the subject of 'academic freedom' only within a broader discussion of 'accountability' and 'responsibility'.)

It is precisely because of this erosion of the conditions necessary for academic freedom, argues Rorty, that the notion is worth defending. For Rorty academic freedom is not a general principle, but a way of naming 'some complicated local folkways that have developed in the course of the past century… These customs and traditions insulate colleges and universities from politics and from public opinion. In particular, they insulate teachers from pressure from the public bodies or private boards who pay their wages' (1996: 21). In the absence of 'nice sharp distinctions between appropriate social utility and inappropriate politicization', he sees the notion of academic freedom as providing some 'pretty fuzzy' distinctions, which may nevertheless be useful in ensuring that universities 'remain healthy and free': 'fuzziness does not, and should not, make us treasure free and independent universities any the less' (p 28).

Another critical response to the traditional version of academic freedom points to tensions between categories of freedom (such as freedom of speech) that have the status of a public right, and categories of freedom (such as academic freedom) that apply exclusively to a subgroup or elite. Can the latter be seen, simply, as a subcategory of the former? Or does the latter, in its exclusivity, challenge the inclusive aspirations of the former? The tensions become particularly apparent when one considers how these different freedoms might be justified. If, as

Haworth (1998: 15) suggests, 'a defense of free speech must treat the right of free speech as a public right – "public" in the sense that it can be exercised by any non-assignable member of the community – and not as exclusive to a subgroup or elite', then any such defence would require a very different kind of rationale than that involved in defending academic freedom. The latter is evoked not as 'a public right' conferred upon the whole people, but as a right conferred upon a particular group of people. Any justification of academic freedom must not only defend that exclusivity, but defend it *in the name of freedom*. Therein lie the tensions and potential contradictions. Can academic freedom ever be anything other than a matter of professional self-interest?

Dworkin (1996) believes it can and in the course of justifying his claim calls for 'a new interpretation of academic freedom'. Like Rorty he believes that 'the conventional, instrumental defense of academic freedom is important, and at least in general valid', but unlike Rorty claims that 'it is not enough'. He goes on to argue 'that academic freedom plays an important ethical role not just in the lives of the few people it protects, but in the life of the community more generally. It is an important, structural part of the culture of independence that we need in order to lead the kind of lives that we should.' The protection of academic freedom, Dworkin seems to be saying, is symbolic of the protection of a more general freedom of which freedom of speech is a crucial component: 'an invasion of academic freedom is insulting and harmful for some because it frustrates satisfying important responsibilities, and it is dangerous for everyone because it weakens the culture of independence and cheapens the ideal that culture protects' (p 187).

Should we, then, jettison the notion of academic freedom altogether? The problem in doing so is, as both Dworkin and Rorty agree, that without it there is no insulation from the vagaries of market forces on the one hand and state intervention on the other. The problem in not doing so is that, in hanging on to it, one may be simply reasserting territorial prerogatives that no longer count for much and that are, anyway, morally questionable in a supposedly egalitarian society. However, argues Dworkin, it is possible to 'reinterpret' academic freedom in such a way that one is able to retain some of its residual value as 'insulation', while ethically realigning it with 'a culture of independence'.

It is difficult not to interpret Dworkin's 'reinterpretation' as an attempt to have one's cake and eat it. Both he and Rorty make interesting points about how academic freedom might be justified, but both are nevertheless committed to maintaining a traditional conception of academic freedom. Their justifications may be innovatory, but what is being justified remains much the same. What is required is not a 'reinterpretation' of academic freedom, but a reorientation of professional values and practices such that academic workers 'use' their academic freedom as *freedom for others*. At the very least, as Horn (1999: 354) puts it, 'professors owe it to themselves and their fellow citizens to use their freedom for the common good'.

Towards a new professionalism

There is no *deus ex machina* to lift us out of what Perkin has analysed as a deeply ingrained professional society, made up of 'career hierarchies of specialised occupations, selected by merit and based on trained expertise' (1989: 2). Such a society, precisely because it has become so deeply professionalized, undoubtedly contains within it contradictory tendencies towards deprofessionalization and deskilling (see, for example, Bottery and Wright, 1996, 1997; Ozga, 1995). The choice, however, is not between a hopelessly compromised professionalism and the return to the grand old days of 'amateurism', but between different versions of professionalism that represent different values and priorities. Indeed, the virtues of 'amateurism', as highlighted by Said (1994) in the 1993 Reith Lectures, constitute the kind of ethical shift that could be seen as a necessary condition for professional renewal: a new professionalism 'fuelled by care and affection rather than by profit, and selfish, narrow specialization' (p 61); a professionalism based not on 'doing what one is supposed to do' but on asking 'why one does it, who benefits from it, how can it reconnect with a personal project and original thoughts' (p 62). Such values prefigure a professional reorientation that requires of its practitioners a willingness to reconceive and radically readjust the relation between their own 'small world' of professional interests and the wider public interests of the world 'out there' (Freidson, 1994; Nixon, 1996, 1997; Nixon *et al*, 1997; Nixon and Ranson, 1997).

Our 'small world' of professional practice encounters the world 'out there' in the form of the students we teach and the wider constituencies that we address through our research and scholarly activity and through our writing. That encounter is framed by a shared concern with learning. One historically resonant expression of this professional ideal is that of the academic as public intellectual whose prime responsibility is to students, colleagues *and* the wider community. The realization of that ideal is through the traditional practices of scholarship and teaching, research and writing. These are the practices whereby the university remains open to difference: difference of opinion and outlook; difference of cultural background and expectation; difference of position and location. Without a respect for and nurturing of these practices as ends in themselves, the university and those who work and study within it will be seriously diminished. The university must reach out in order to survive.

But it must reach out on the basis of a clear recognition of its traditional strengths and responsibilities. The marketization of university education has led to an increased emphasis on quality control. In an attempt to ensure quality, successive governments have actively encouraged certain kinds of research rather than others, have promoted 'innovation' in teaching as an end in itself and have failed to recognize or reward the kinds of routine scholarly activities that inform and characterize both teaching and research in higher education. Moreover, they have done this by encouraging competition between and within institutions (in spite of an 'official' emphasis on collaboration and collegiality). So we are not talking here about any old 'reaching out', but a 'reaching out' based upon particular kinds of values: the values of care and affection, of critical engagement and dialogue, of public concern and welfare. And these are not, of course, the values of the market-place.

The moral basis of the new professionalism lies, then, in our recognition of the freedom of *all*, academics included, to learn and to go on learning. It is the prime responsibility of the academic profession to protect and uphold that freedom. In reminding us of the implications of this responsibility, Walker (1998) highlights the importance of a social justice agenda for the new professionalism: 'The ethical turn must, then, also be a political turn framed by the society we would hope to build, a concern for oppressed and marginalised groups, and a reflexive recognition of the ways in which universities perpetuate relationships of power and domination, even while they challenge them.' Academics, she goes on to argue, will always be awkwardly placed in relation to the institutions of higher education within which they practise: 'We may prefer not to imagine, and indeed to forget, how universities have played a critical role in the construction of a consumer society, of monopoly capitalism, and the rise of the middle class. More recently, universities persist in a complicated positioning, which does not easily or comfortably map onto a radical agenda for education, in late capitalist society' (p 293).

In addressing these points, the new professionalism must not only look beyond its own professional and institutional interests, but must also take a critical look at those interests and at the moral and political assumptions that underpin them. It must in short be both oppositional and self-critical.

The 'commodification of higher education', as Shumar (1997) has analysed it, has become such a part of academic culture and professional discourse that academics may not readily realize the extent to which they are implicated in it. Halsey (1995: 305) has written that it was not until he had read hundreds of responses from academics to a survey of the changing conditions of higher education that he realized how 'the rhetoric of business models and market relations – the language of customers, competition, efficiency gains, "value for money", etc. – could be so totally substituted for relations of trust'. If this mindset is to be challenged, it must therefore be challenged reflexively, with a self-critical eye to the way in which our own values and practices are implicated in that which we are challenging.

The task of professional reconstruction outlined above is daunting. This chapter provides no blueprint, but it does offer some preliminary thoughts on what it might mean to redefine our academic practices and purposes in terms of a reorientation of academic freedom towards *freedom for others*:

- *Redefining what counts as research.* It would mean that research must be seen as central to academic life, but that restrictive definitions of research that currently dominate the academic scene would be broadened and democratized. If the academic life is about learning (one's own *and* others'), then research must be at the forefront. But for learning to be seen in research-active terms (rather than as the passive receipt and retransmission of other people's 'findings'), a more inclusive and differentiated notion of research needs to be developed and articulated: in short, modes of empirical inquiry and reflexive theorizing that currently fall outside the conventional categories urgently require recognition. Academics would need to pursue their own research, encourage and support the research of others (including that of their students and colleagues), *and* redefine the parameters of what counts as research within their own field. In so doing they would almost certainly seek to challenge the mechanisms (such as competitive bidding and the Research Assessment Exercise) whereby research is currently funded through the Research Councils and, since the 1992 Further and Higher Education Reform Act, through the Higher Education Funding Councils for England (HEFCE), Scotland (SHEFC) and Wales (HEFCW). They would also seek to challenge and redefine the priorities of academic publishing houses, many of which collude in the promotion of academic writing that is addressed to increasingly specialized and exclusive readerships (see Jacoby, 1997; Nixon, 1999).
- *Putting the teaching relationship first.* It would mean, also, that teaching relationships would form, and to a great extent frame, the professional identity of the academic worker. 'Are our universities ignoring undergraduate education?' is a key question posed by a recent work on the future of the US university (Duderstadt, 2000: 81). It is also a crucial question for many institutions of higher education within the UK, where evidence is mounting of the deleterious effect on university teaching of research selectivity funding mechanisms (see, for example, McNay, 1998; Segal Quince Wicksteed Limited, 1996). Currently the experience of one-to-one tuition, or even of small-group discussion, is virtually restricted to postgraduate research students (and, even for this group, it is by no means assured). It is difficult to see how student learning can be prioritized without some radical reversal of this current set of circumstances. However, that reversal cannot be at the expense of opening up access and equalizing opportunities. The kind of professional paradigm we are trying to imagine would both privilege the student–teacher relationship (particularly through small-group discussion and tuition) and open up access through an increasingly varied further and higher education sector catering for people of all ages and different circumstances.
- *Developing our professional selves.* It would mean the reintegration of professional development. The trend is increasingly towards 'staff development' or

'academic development' units that are often tangential to the broader faculty structure that they seek to 'service'. In the UK these units may even be defined as 'non-academic', which leads to the absurd situation whereby 'non-academics' are given responsibility for developing 'academic' professionalism. 'There is now, in higher education,' as Evans and Abbott (1998: 15) point out, 'a large industry involving an increasing number of full-time staff trainers who have responsibility for improving tutors' performance in various areas of their work.' If, as academic workers, we were to become serious about our own professionalism, then we would ensure that the task of professional development was clearly located within the academic structures of higher education, preferably at department or faculty level. We would see professional development as professional *self*-development, in other words, and take responsibility for it as such. Not to take responsibility in this way represents a failure of professional nerve that is self-defeating and that weakens the core relations upon which the professional identity of academics ought to depend.

- *Turning collegiality inside out.* It would mean redrawing the boundaries of academic collegiality and ensuring openness and transparency in our professional dealings with one another. 'Collegiality' is one of those words ('loyalty' is another) that often mask complex power relations and the manipulative and sometimes exploitative practices to which these can give rise. Within hierarchical institutions collegiality can be used to ensure horizontal power bases at different levels within the system: deans dine together, heads of department hobnob, professors conspire, etc. There is, admittedly, a downward trickle, whereby 'promising' academics are admitted socially to a higher level on the tacit assumption all round that they are headed there anyway. But in the main collegiality in higher education is anything but collegial. So the ethical turn would mean, first, greater transparency in our dealings with one another (How exactly did he get that external examining post? Why was she given that particular departmental responsibility?) and, second, an attempt to forge mutually supportive relationships against the grain of institutional hierarchies, sector-wide inequalities of race and gender, and the discriminatory practices to which these hierarchies and inequalities give rise.
- *Recognizing disciplinary differences.* Finally, it would mean recognizing and respecting disciplinary and subject differences. Inter-disciplinarity does not mean the dissolution of such differences; on the contrary, inter-disciplinary practice depends upon a recognition of, and respect for, the cultural, epistemological and methodological differences between disciplinary and subject areas. Collaborative ventures that are not grounded in these principles of mutual recognition and respect are likely to be anything but collaborative. Indeed, they are almost certain to reinforce existing hierarchies and ensure the continuing dominance of traditional paradigms. Inter-disciplinarity is only as

good as the disciplinary traditions that sustain it. This is particularly the case when considering the relation between teaching and research. That some such relation exists should, arguably, be a condition of higher education. But the way in which natural scientists relate their research to their teaching may be very different from the way in which historians or modern languages specialists set about this task. Moreover, whilst research *into* teaching may be a valuable activity for some (particularly those in education departments), it is not for most academics the way in which their teaching relates to their research. Nor should it be (although the fashionable emphasis placed by the staff development industry on 'action research' and 'reflective practice' would seem to suggest otherwise).

Concluding comments

It is through the broad, inclusive traditions of scholastic endeavour that the idea of the university struggled for and found its precarious position within a secular, civil society: a tradition founded in the routines of the examined life, but increasingly carried forward, as Damrosch reminds us, through 'intellectual sociability' (1995: 186) and a principled rejection of the idea of 'the scholar as isolated individual' (p 188). The choice is *not*, as so often presented, between the alienation of the ivory tower and the managerialism of the bureaucratically accountable institution. There are other ways implicit in the practices and traditions of scholastic life whereby academics, students and the communities of which they are a part can learn to work together, think together, talk together *for the common good*. What needs to be renewed and sustained is a broad, inclusive tradition of scholarship that privileges the notion of the examined life and that, as Said remarks, takes us beyond ourselves: 'You will have other things to think about and enjoy than merely yourself and your domain, and those other things are far more impressive, far more worthy of study and respect than self-adulation and uncritical self-appreciation. To join the academic world is therefore to enter a ceaseless quest for knowledge and freedom' (1996: 228).

6

Teaching, research and scholarship: the role of professional development

Introduction

There are three areas that will be addressed in this chapter. First, consideration is given to the role of professional development within the context of scholarship and the implications for the academic in higher education. Second, consideration is given to the concept of *scholarship* and the role teaching and research have within it. I explain how it will be used in the discussion and place it firmly within the context of learning. The notion put forward is that academic teaching has a significant role to play in academics' own learning and that within higher education the responsibility for this must lie with the academics themselves. I argue that it is more timely now than ever before in higher education to think in terms of the 'scholarship of teaching'.

Professional development and professionalism

It is important to this discussion to clarify some of the meanings of the various terms associated with professional development, as they have come to mean a variety of things to those associated with education. Watkins and Drury (1994) suggest that there are four groups of strategies for the development of professionals over the next decade:

1. developing a new mindset;
2. learning to promote and market one's skills, networking and cultivating relationships;
3. developing self-insight and taking personal charge;
4. developing a range of competencies.

These four dimensions define for me the role of professional development in higher education at the present time. They highlight areas that can move individuals towards considering themselves as professionals and take on board a form of professionality that focuses on the quality of practice in context. Such practice requires radically altered relations of power and control (Nixon, 1996: 12). Thus, highlighting the need for a 'learning profession', Nixon suggests that while 'professionalism has always been ideological, what is new about the emergent professionalism is that, under complex and competing pressures, it has become openly and explicitly so... Underlying practices of the emergent teacher professionalism, then, is a set of professional codes, which has the potential for integrating teaching and learning, curriculum and assessment in new and exciting ways' (pp 6–7).

   The above statement clearly explains the changes occurring in both the compulsory, and more recently, the higher education sectors. Debates in higher education, both nationally and internationally, have increasingly placed teaching at the centre of effective student learning, with the premise that good teaching leads to effective learning. There is nothing new in this statement alone. However, what it is important to recognize is that it is a relatively new dimension in higher education, where research has through tradition always been the key word and centre of activity. For new academics the concept of learning to teach and gaining an understanding of the theory related to teaching requires a new mindset. Brew suggests that notwithstanding the many changes that have taken place in higher education there is still considerable resistance among many academics to changing their teaching (1999: 294). However, the new mindset that Brew refers to is gradually being addressed through induction programmes on teaching and learning across the higher education sector. But if such programmes are to be effective, the ideas related to learning, and learning from learning, for academics need to be explored.

The case for teaching as scholarship

The practice of teaching in higher education and the role of learning for the academic are equally dependent on the whole educational context, particularly now when universities are facing periods of rapid change. For higher education, this means considering how teaching is going to affect the role of learning for the academic in pursuit of new knowledge. This then brings the notion of teaching as scholarship and its role within a research-based university centre stage. It also suggests the question: why should academics be motivated to become good teachers? This is an important question to consider, bearing in mind that most promotions still rely on research publications and meeting the demands of the RAE.

Why or maybe how is it that scholarship is tied closely to research rather than teaching and is there a mechanism for changing these ideas? Nelson called for the renewal of the teacher-scholar, much like academics in the earlier decades of the 20th century. Nelson describes the ideal teacher-scholar in the following way:

> Ideally the college professor would be a widely respected scholar excited about learning and capable of communicating this excitement to others, a teacher deeply concerned with welfare of students and eager to have them learn and grow, one who teaches imaginatively both by books and by personal example, a demanding very compassionate person who respects the moral worth of students and their potential growth.
>
> (Nelson, 1981: 7)

However, present-day conceptions of scholarship are much too narrow. Increasingly the literature is arguing that there is a need to reconceptualize the meaning of scholarship within higher education. Rice suggests that during the expansion period in US higher education, what Jencks and Riesman (1968) called the 'academic revolution', scholarship was equated with research and the cutting edge of a discipline. Further, it took on significance only when it was publishable in a refereed journal – one narrow facet of the scholarly enterprise, one way of knowing (Rice, 1992: 115).

In today's globalized society, with an ever-increasing need for knowledge, academics need to perceive scholarship in a wider context, which allows for diversity and accepts the expanding and changing demands of higher education. This is a view of scholarship that embraces the day-to-day working lives of the new generation of academics, and one that very much includes teaching.

'Scholarship' has increasingly returned to our vocabulary in higher education, but not in the context of teaching. Teaching is considered by many as a derivative activity. The ideal teacher-scholar as described by Nelson was and is not the norm. At this juncture it is relevant to consider how the professionalization of the scholar has influenced the concept of scholarship being associated with research rather than teaching. Nixon discusses this in considerable detail in Chapter 5. Parsons (1968), in an essay on the professions, described the 'educational revolution' that was occurring post-World War II. Fundamental to this revolution was the process of professionalization. Central to his argument was that a professionally orientated society needs the modern university, and 'the professional *par excellence* is the academic'. Parsons defines this excellent academic thus: 'The typical professor now resembles the scientist more that the gentleman-scholar of earlier times. As a result of the process of professionalisation, achievement criteria are now given the highest priority, reputations are established in national and international forums rather than locally defined, and centre of gravity has shifted to the graduate faculties and their newly professionalised large-scale research function' (1968: 52).

Although describing the US case, Parsons's description is equally appropriate to what is happening in Britain today. This notion of research excellence is extenuated in Britain through the Research Assessment Exercise. However, what is interesting about Parsons's statement is that it does not describe the typical professor. Rice (1992) suggests that what Parsons articulates is 'the dominant fiction by which typical American [and I would argue all] professors measure themselves and their colleagues as professionals'. Rice goes on to argue that the image of the academic professor shaped the conceptions of a faculty and institutional policies to the extent that it determined promotion, tenure and sabbaticals. This perception of the academic remains and is at present dominant in higher education.

Finally Rice (1992: 119) articulates seven criteria that dominate the professional image of the academic:

1. Research is the central professional endeavour and the focus of academic life.
2. Quality in the profession is maintained by peer review and professional autonomy.
3. Knowledge is pursued for its own sake.
4. The pursuit of knowledge is best organized according to discipline (ie according to discipline-based departments).
5. Reputations are established through national and international professional associations.
6. The distinctive task of the academic professional is the pursuit of cognitive truth.
7. Professional rewards and mobility accrue to those who persistently accentuate their specialization.

The above criteria are now well established and recognizable as elements of the academic's life. However, are they correct criteria by which academic development should be judged? I would like to argue that they are not. We are now at a juncture in higher education that requires a broader conception of scholarship, one that facilitates the development of an academic in the broadest sense.

The work of Ernest Boyer and more recently the scholarship of teaching and learning framework produced by the Carnegie Foundation (1999) are a way of considering development projects that can assist in elevating the status of teaching within higher education through inclusive programmes, not imposed development.

Boyer was one of the first to draw attention to the narrow conception of scholarship held by the profession. He stated: 'Scholarship is not an esoteric appendage; it is at the heart of what the profession is all about. All faculty, throughout their careers, should themselves remain students. As scholars they must continue to learn and be seriously and continuously engaged in the expanding intellectual world. This is essential to the vitality and vigour of the undergraduate college' (1987: 67).

Given this emphasis on learning, the need to continue to learn should be key to the notion of scholarship, particularly in relation to teaching as scholarship. Shulman (1993) expanded Boyer's views by inferring that teaching could be made more scholarly if it became public property. By this he meant that we could publicly document and assess teaching in powerful ways (see Chew, in Chapter 6) and, as a consequence, teaching itself would become more scholarly in every sense of the term.

Boyer's analysis of scholarship identified four key roles: the scholarship of teaching, of discovery, of application and of integration. He considered teaching not simply as a matter of dissemination or transmission of knowledge, but as a form of scholarship, by which he meant transforming and extending knowledge through the process of classroom debate and a continual examination and challenge of both content and pedagogy.

Before considering the implications of Boyer's four forms of scholarship, it is important to reflect on Boyer's own beliefs: 'We acknowledge that these four – the scholarship of discovery, of integration, of application and of teaching – divide intellectual functions that are tied inseparably to each other. Still there is value, we believe, in analysing the various kinds of academic work, while also acknowledging that they dynamically interact, formatting an independent whole' (1990: 25).

Boyer's assertion allows us to look at scholarship in a broader context, thus allowing scholarship to be viewed as an interrelated whole with distinctive components and different approaches to knowing. Figure 6.1 shows an enlarged view of scholarly work.

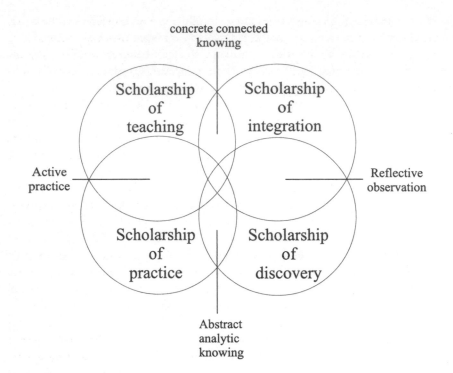

Figure 6.1 An enlarged view of scholarly work

The four forms of scholarship

Boyer emphasized the scholarship of discovery, or research, as a 'pervasive process of intellectual excitement' rather than just a concern with outcomes in the form of new knowledge. However, Boyer also realized that the extension of the frontiers of knowledge was not enough, and that academics needed to be constantly involved in the interpretation of knowledge. This allowed for connections between knowledge and models from different disciplines to be made. It requires a divergent approach to knowing. The scholarship of application was defined as professional activity in practice and service, which had to be subject to the rigour of evaluation and accountability as teaching and research.

Finally, and most important to this chapter, is the scholarship of teaching. Boyer suggests that the scholarship of teaching has integrity of its own, but is deeply embedded in the other three forms. The particular characteristics are: 1) its *synoptic capacity*, the ability to draw the strands of a field together in a way that provides both coherence and meaning; 2) *pedagogical content knowledge*, the capacity to represent a subject in ways that transcend the split between intellectual substance and teaching process; 3) *what we know about learning*, scholarly inquiry into how students 'make meaning' out of what teachers say and do.

The scholarship of teaching is perceived as an inclusive activity. This perspective suggests that academics take a scholarly approach to teaching by reflecting on the knowledge gained from educational research in relation to particular contexts in which they teach. It emphasizes the important reciprocal relationship that exists between theory and practice, and the value of the practitioners' experienced-based knowledge.

It is important to state here that we are not advocating all teaching be turned into research for it to count as scholarship. On the contrary, I would wish to advocate that the scholarship of teaching involves learning about teaching and demonstrating that knowledge in practice, reflecting Mezirow's (1992) theory of transformative learning through three levels of reflection, each generating a different kind of knowledge: reflection on content, processes and premise. This puts the emphasis on learning from the perspective of both the student and the academic. Mezirow is returned to in Chapter 7, where a framework for future professional development is suggested. However, at this juncture it is important to move the discussion forward. Following on the argument of teaching and scholarship necessitates looking at the academic as a learner, when it comes to teaching. For this reason we need to consider the implications of an academic being an adult learner in the workplace.

Considering the academic as an adult learner

Possible ways forward can be found in the theories related to adult learning and change in organizations. These theories suggest that relationships between specific dimensions of the workplace and learning can allow learning and environment to be perceived as multidimensional concepts. This in turn obliges us to consider the types of environment that allow the academic to learn, and the conditions under which that learning can be promoted.

An analysis of the literature (for example, Brookfield, 1991; Merriam and Caffarella, 1991; Jarvis, 1996) suggests that there are five distinct themes relating to adult learners, which are exemplified below:

1. Adults learn and have the potential to learn throughout their lives (Jarvis, 1992).
2. Adult learning may occur across settings and circumstances (Marsick and Watkins, 1990).
3. Adult learners enter learning situations with prior knowledge, beliefs and skills (Knowles, 1984) and these may affect their learning (Moll, 1990).
4. Adult learners are problem-oriented, and learning occurs when the problem is related in a meaningful way to the adult's life situation; what Jarvis (1986) refers to as the impetus for learning comes from conflict between personal 'biography' and current experience. This suggests that learning will not take place unless a problem implicates routine practice or taken-for-granted knowledge.
5. Adults can play a very active role in their own learning. Knowles (1984) suggests that adults are also proactive and self-directed in searching for new learning opportunities.

If adults are capable of learning in this way, consideration must be given to the type of learning that should be promoted in the case of an academic. It is also important to understand how academics view their learning in relation to knowledge about their discipline. Brew suggests that if 'academics view knowledge as a product of communication and negotiation, the link between research and teaching becomes intimate' (1999: 296). This implies moving towards a pluralistic view of knowledge, one that fully takes on board the interpretative nature of academic work. This then allows research and teaching to be seen as being in a symbiotic relationship. Research (Smeby, 1998; Rowland, 1996) shows that academics' views and their criteria for determining what is research and what is teaching are determined by the intellectual level of the audience. Although this view acknowledges that teaching is linked with scholarship it does not reflect assertions by Elton (1986, 1992), Westergraad (1991) and Neumann (1993) that teaching and research are related by the common activity of scholarship. Elton defines scholarship as the interpretation of what is already known, the primary work that feeds into all things academics are supposed to do, whilst Neumann extends the concept of scholarship to include the idea of quality, by describing the way in which the inquiry should be done. Scholarship, she says, should be 'used in two ways in the academic community: first to describe an activity that extends into many roles of academic work, and second, to describe a quality, or mode of working' (p 103).

Rice reinforces this notion of teaching as scholarship by suggesting: 'The scholarship of teaching has a distinctive symbiotic capacity, that is the ability to draw the strands of a field together in a way that provides both coherence and meaning, to place what is known in context and open the way for connections to be made between knower and the known' (1992: 73). The inference here is that to teach well academics must understand what they have learnt from their research before this can adequately be assimilated and taught. 'Quality teaching requires substantive scholarship that builds on, but is distinct from original research' (1992: 125).

How can this help the development of the academic?

Accepting that there is a connection between the knower and the known enables academics to draw on data, ideas or theories taken from their research projects and present them in a coherent and meaningful way to themselves and their students. It is also essential that academics understand how best to teach the concepts and ideas of the research. Glew (1992) presents such a view and states that 'research can transform the teaching/learning experience, reflecting the contribution research can make to teaching and learning'. But what of the contribution teaching has to make to research and learning?

Earlier it was suggested that there is a symbiotic relationship between research and teaching. Accepting this notion is an essential step forward to changing attitudes towards teaching and learning and the role professional development has to play within that change process. Recognizing such a relationship can help create an environment in which researchers have to plan a presentation of their research in a simple and coherent way for the purpose of teaching. This helps expose weakness in the research through the delivery of the material, and therefore requires academics to modify the presentation. This is good practice if researchers understand the process of teaching and learning that they have been involved in.

Teaching should enable academics to place their area of research into a broader context and not just be confined to their specific, narrow area of specialism. The academics thus benefit from reviewing their section of their discipline and placing their own work within the wider context of the discipline as a whole. This type of reflexive process can help answer what Rowland considers a significant question for academics: 'to consider how their understanding of the nature of learning [from their disciplinary standpoint] relates to their practice as teachers and learners' (1999: 312).

However, improved teaching and learning will only occur if researchers have the knowledge and skills to reflect on these processes and change accordingly. This requires academics to develop a capacity for the type of reflection that allows them to learn from their research and enhance learning, and to be able to relay this learning to their students, that is learn from their own learning. Jarvis (1999) argues that practitioners must engage in developing theory from practice if they are to learn from learning and develop a meaningful practice. If this form of engagement occurs, then the quality of teaching and learning will truly improve.

For teaching to improve and be valued, there needs to be a relationship between professional development, learning and the scholarship of teaching, or as Boyatzis, Cowan and Knolb (1995) suggest, the scholarship of learning. However, there is a problem here, in that assessment has centred on the quality of learning, with no prescriptive model of good teaching being offered to ensure its achievement. Teaching in this context has been taken to cover a range of activities that involve the learner either passively or actively in some form of activity, on the assumption that learning will be associated with that activity. The connection between the 'teaching' and the learner is often not understood by the academic. What is required, therefore, is for academics to understand the teaching and learning process, as dictated by their discipline, by which I mean the process of understanding the impact of pedagogic practice of the teaching and learning of the particular discipline the academic is involved in. This then becomes the connecting element between professional development and learning. After all, academics, through the university process, aim to help students learn by changing the way they think. Is it not then reasonable to expect academics to be well versed in the same process, ie changing the way they think about the teaching/learning process? Development of this kind is a powerful route to professional learning, as it engages the individual in the type of learning and scholarship Greetz (1980) refers to as 'fundamental change in the way we think about the way we think'.

Learners, in this case academics, have to be at the centre of the professional development programme. Whilst learners are key in this process, the programmes are often crafted ahead of time by the educators, based on their knowledge and model of the academic learner. This model is frequently rooted in what they believe about how professionals, in this case academics, incorporate knowledge into practice, under what conditions they learn best and what role prior experience plays in learning.

These models and preconceptions are so deeply embedded in educational educators that they often tend to act implicitly. With the imposition of professional development in teaching and learning, it becomes ever more necessary for educators to consider how best academics learn and which model or models fit their needs. This is a difficult assertion to deal with, especially if we believe that professionals learn in many ways and that the forms of learning differ according to desired ends. Bruner puts this eloquently when he says that 'there is no completely naturalistic way of resolving the question about what model we want to enshrine at the centre of our practice of education... At the heart of the decision process there must be a value judgement about how the mind should be cultivated and to what end' (1985: 5).

What is now needed is to construct a model of professional learning for the academic that is consistent with the critical viewpoint. This critical viewpoint, I suggest, should be 'enshrined at the centre of our practice' of professional development. The key premise of this statement is that practice itself, and even more importantly the reflection that should go side by side with practice, are the most fruitful sources of development.

Now is the time educators should be considering and taking into account the ways in which academics develop their knowledge of teaching, learning, scholarship and research through their practice. Programmes should facilitate learning through the disciplines' base. Generic issues are also very important, but academics are led by their discipline, not generic issues. As such, programmes must and should facilitate learning to the extent that academics begin to understand the scholarship of teaching their discipline.

Examples of using the scholarship of teaching, as a means of thinking about professional development: a discipline-based approach

The ILT is looking to improve the quality of teaching in higher education and, as previously stated, is attempting to do this by accrediting training courses within higher education institutions. Yet if you go into any university library and look at the books on teaching and learning, you will see a catalogue of teaching schemes, approaches and projects that have been attempted and fallen into obscurity. So why is it that there is this belief that another set of literature or courses will change the quality of teaching and learning in higher education?

Much of the work carried out by educational developers and educational development units in higher education targets individuals. The underlying assumption for this targeting appears to be based on the notion that equipping the individual with new skills and attitudes will eventually lead to improved practice and higher-quality learning and teaching. Added to this assumption is the belief or hope that, through the process of equipping individuals with new skills, the newly developed individual will be able to influence colleagues, and thus bring about further change in learning and teaching quality. Research shows that more often than not this does not occur, with new-found enthusiasm eroding and old habits resurfacing on return to the department or school.

What needs to be considered here, which as a consequence will have a bearing on future professional development, is that teaching and learning need to be perceived and understood in an academic and scholarly way. It needs to be accepted that education is a discipline in its own right. Teaching is still looked upon as an intuitive practice. Appreciating that learning and understanding are the main goals of teaching, and that learning and understanding are multifaceted, promoted by a variety of teaching activities, takes more than description of teaching activities or tips for surviving lectures. Learning and teaching have to be perceived as more scholarly by making them more public property.

How can we as academics begin to understand what it means to improve teaching and learning, and cause this understanding to become public property? A classic example of how a scholarly approach to teaching can be applied is that of the famous physicist Richard Feynman.

The case of Richard Feynman, physicist and scholar

Professor Stephen Chew, Samford University, USA
A prototypical example of the scholarly nature of remarkable teaching is found in the career of physicist Richard Feynman. James Gleick's (1992) biography, *Genius: The life and science of Richard Feynman*, describes how Feynman was asked to update and redesign the introductory physics course sequence at Caltech. Gleick describes the status of the course when Feynman was asked to redesign it. The description can be applied to most fields and far too many courses taught today.

> The course had grown stale. Too much ancient pedagogy lingered in it...
> The pace of change in modern science had accelerated as most college syllabuses had hardened. It was no longer possible, as it had been a generation before, to bring undergraduates up to the live frontier of a field like physics or biology. Yet if quantum mechanics or molecular genetics could not be integrated into undergraduate education, science risked becoming a historical subject.
>
> (Gleick, 1992: 357–58)

So what is it that Feynman did that can help with issues today?

Feynman began by redesigning his course by the enduring understanding he wanted to convey to students. In archived documents at Caltech a summary of Feynman's teaching philosophy shows that he asked himself some very fundamental questions, prior to designing and implementing his foundations of physics courses. 'First figure out why you want the students to learn the subject and what you want them to know, and the method will result more or less by common sense' (Feynman, 1952, cited in Goodstein and Neugebauer, 1989).

Feynman's first lecture began as follows:

If, in some cataclysm, all of scientific knowledge were destroyed, and only one sentence passed on to the next generation of creatures, what statement would contain the most information in the fewest words? I believe it is the *atomic hypothesis*... that *all things are made of atoms – little particles that move around in perpetual motion, attracting each other when they are a little distance apart, but repelling upon being squeezed into one another*. In that one sentence, you will see, there is an *enormous* amount of information about the world, if just a little imagination and thinking are applied.

(Feynman, Leighton and Sands, 1963: 1–2)

The rest of Feynman's course was spent explicating or 'uncovering' this fundamental concept. In Gleick's biography of Feynman he states that 'this was the world of Feynman. No scientist since Newton had so ambitiously and unconventionally set down the full measure of his knowledge of world – his own knowledge and his community's... The course was a magisterial achievement: word was spreading through the scientific community even before it ended' (Gleick, 1992: 363). Feynman's new course revolutionized the teaching of physics and was published as *The Feynman Lectures on Physics* (Feynman, Leighton and Sands, 1963).

What is important here to this example is consideration of the scholarship required to teach this course. Gleick states that 'teaching was only one of the [Feynman's] goals. He realized also that he wished to organise whole embracing knowledge of physics, to turn it end over until he could find all the interconnections that were usually, he believed left as loose ends. He felt as though he were making a map' (Gleick, 1992: 358). There could not be a clearer example of Boyer's (1990) scholarship of integration. Gleick makes a distinction between teaching and integration, but the distinction is a false one. Any teacher designing a new course has to integrate information to create a meaningful and accessible whole for students. Finally, Gleick states that Feynman 'found that he was working harder than at any time since the atomic bomb project' (Gleick, 1992: 358). This statement is especially striking because during the period since the development of the atomic bomb, Feynman had conducted his Nobel Prize-winning work on quantum electrodynamics.

How could anyone dispute that Feynman's teaching was a significant act of scholarship? The problem of teaching effectively the introductory physics course, or virtually any course, is as ill-structured and challenging as most problems in traditional research. Feynman brought the same knowledge, insight, ability, creativity, in short the same brain, to bear on his problem as on his traditional research. The course was publicly documented as a book and, in terms of assessment, it has influenced the way physics is taught and understood by a generation of physicists and lay people.

Feynman's lectures found their audience among other physicists who appreciated his accomplishment, but how did the students in the course fare? Feynman himself was pessimistic. In his preface to the published lectures, he noted what he called a 'very serious difficulty' with the whole experience: 'there wasn't any feedback from the students to the lecturer to indicate how well the lectures were going over'. Without such feedback, he said, 'I don't know how good the lectures really are'. He summed up his overall evaluation of the lectures this way: 'My own point of view – which, however, does not seem to be shared by most people who worked with the students – is pessimistic. I don't think I did very well by the students. When I look at the way the majority of the students handled the problems on the examinations, I think that the system was a failure' (Feynman, Leighton and Sands, 1963: 5).

To Feynman, if the students didn't learn and understand, then his lectures were a failure, regardless of how brilliant the lectures were. How simple it would have been to conclude that because he had put so much work into the lectures, and because other physicists recognized their merit, it must be the students' problem if they did not learn. This was the only time he ever taught these courses, but in the preface he notes, 'Maybe I'll have a chance to do it again someday. Then I'll do it right.'

The Feynman episode provides an instinctive example of the scholarship of teaching. Good teaching requires a tremendous amount of integration of research ideas, which is then translated into learning activities that promote a coherent understanding on the part of the student. A well-developed course is an implementation of both one's theory of the field and how best to train the thinking of students. The best teaching reflects the teacher's conception of the discipline, but judged by what the students learn in the field. The teacher must separate the timeless from the merely fashionable in terms of ideas and pedagogy. Therefore, to be effective, teaching must change as rapidly as the field and it must also undergo continuous refinement in light of what the students are or are not learning. No course is ever fully developed. Like traditional research, a course merely represents our best understanding thus far, and is always subject to revision. In traditional research, we never assume that we know all there is to know about a phenomenon, and there are many examples of phenomena that were thought to be well understood only to have new research give fresh insight and perspective. Why then do we ever consider courses finished and complete in their development?

Implications from the case of Feynman

Chew's example and subsequent argument of Feynman have significant implications when considering the professional development of new academics. What is it that we want new academics to learn and understand about teaching and learning in higher education? Is it merely the giving of information as a means of meeting the demands of a teaching role, or is it to enhance and develop deep learning and understanding of specific disciplines? One would hope it is the latter.

It is clear from the above example that to teach well requires a good and deep understanding of one's discipline, but it requires something else, that is an understanding of what it is to develop teaching materials and create learning environments by applying similar methodologies to teaching and learning as academics do in their research. As Chew quite correctly states, in research we never assume that we have all the knowledge or that we understand all the knowledge we possess. Why is it that in higher education these assumptions are frequently forgotten when designing and developing courses, and teaching students? What exactly does the Feynman example tell us with respect to professional development?

First, academics must realize the importance of their teaching role, and understand that teaching needs to be explicit, and is accountable. Second, teaching is a scholarly activity, and as such worthy of time being spent on its preparation. Third, a scholarly approach and view to teaching allow failure and unsuccessful learning situations to be evaluated in much the same way as unsuccessful research activities. Finally, although innovative teaching methodologies may be risk-taking, the benefits can be very rewarding by increased student participation and enhanced learning environments.

How a discipline-based approach may help

When faced with the task of exploring new learning problems in their field, academics usually begin by following disciplinary models of development, as in the case of Feynman. Examples can be found in other disciplines. Mary Huber, a senior scholar of the Carnegie Foundation, cites such examples from the American Association of Higher Education (AAHE) course portfolio project. A major outcome from this project shows how disciplines influence thinking about teaching and learning. Huber gives the following example, based on work carried out by Cerbin:

> The very origin of the idea of documenting the unfolding of a single course from conception to result through an analogy to investigate traditions of his discipline, psychology. 'I began to think of each course as a kind of laboratory – not as a truly controlled experiment, of course, but as a setting in which you start out with goals for student learning, then you adopt teaching practices that you think will accomplish these, and along

the way you can watch and see if your practices are helping to accomplish your goals, collecting evidence about effects and impact... the course portfolio is really like a scholarly manuscript... a draft of on going inquiry.'

(Huber, 1999: 53)

Clearly this above extract demonstrates how the disciplinary style empowers the scholarship of teaching. It gives the academic a ready-made way of perceiving and conceptualizing the problem. It also gives academics the parameters by which the problem can be tackled and a choice of methodologies by which to execute the task. It demonstrates that teaching is not just a technique. Shulman (1999) argues that 'teaching is not just a technique but an enhancement, rather, of our understanding of our disciplinary, interdisciplinary or professional field and what it means to know deeply'.

Conceptualizing professional development through the disciplines requires a theoretical framework. Schwab's distinction between the substantive and syntactic structures of a discipline helps this conceptualization. His distinction relates first to the conception that guides inquiry in a discipline (1964: 25), and second to the pathways of inquiry a discipline or small group of disciplines use – what they mean by verified knowledge and how they go about this verification (1964: 21). In other words, when we look at scholarly projects on teaching and learning, we can ask how they have been informed by substantive and syntactic structures from the authors' own fields. In terms of the role of professional development this means facilitating academics' understanding of substantive issues. This means transforming a 'problem' one has encountered in the classroom into a 'problem' for study, ie a problem that has some conceptualization, thought and literature behind it (Bass, 1999).

The distinction between substantive and syntactic issues allows us to consider a variety of activities, related to professional development, that will encourage academics to involve themselves in inquiry within their everyday roles and responsibilities, for example logging the development of a course, programme or set of teaching activities. If academics decide to embark on the design of a new course with the specific intention of testing a set of assumptions about new ways of teaching and learning in their discipline, such as introducing new technologies in combination with other pedagogies and methods, then that helps to identify the complexities of the discipline in an accessible way for the students who are new to the subject. Academics should consider two key aspects that should be logged in the development of such an innovation: the 'pedagogical intentions' and an intensive examination of the evidence collected on student learning. This allows in-depth reflection on the experiment both in the context of academics' own personal and professional development and as a contribution to the field of teaching that particular discipline.

Exploring student learning and indicators of student learning based in one's discipline is another way of using the scholarship of teaching as a means of professional development. Often academics are interested in student evaluations only from the perspective of whether or not their teaching has been successful in the eyes of their students. However, if the academic sets as an aim 'learner-centred' evaluation, this means setting the aim of the evaluation as a way of identifying whether, and to what extent, students have grasped the key concepts that have been taught throughout the session or course. Here a different approach needs to be taken: it requires reflecting on the learning not just the teaching. The academic has to ask questions relating to learning, such as: have the concepts been understood, and if not, why not? Which aspects have not been understood? How can this be rectified? These types of questions then move the emphasis from proving the teaching was successful to uncovering problematic areas and aspects of the teaching–learning process and exploring the identified issues.

All the examples cited above require academics to be more reflective about learning, and also to take risks, including risks to their own values and beliefs, much as they would do in the research and scholarly activities related to their own discipline-based research.

The notion of risk in professional development

This notion of risk is an important one to the discussion of the role of professional development with respect to teaching, learning and scholarship. Fox (1999) puts forward a useful conceptualization of hazards and risk that allows us to consider the risk academics may have to take if the enhancement of teaching through scholarship is to take place. Fox argues that 'risks (hazards) are socially constructed: created from the contingent judgements about the adverse or undesirable outcomes of choices made by human beings. These "hazards" are then invoked discursively to support estimations of risk, risky behaviour and of the people who take the risks' (1999: 19).

What does this mean for academics wanting to develop their teaching? Let us consider the issue of a new academic wishing to introduce new technologies into a particularly conservative department that believes lectures are the accepted form of delivery. The introduction of new technologies does not in itself constitute a threat. New technologies as a teaching strategy only become a risk under certain circumstances, principally if conditions arise such that the new technologies do not function or students cannot participate in the session. We know that such a situation is risky, not through some 'natural' quality of this situation, but because we appraise it as undesired or adverse, based on information from student evaluations and heads of faculty expectations of 'good teaching practice'. This cycle is illustrated in Figure 6.2.

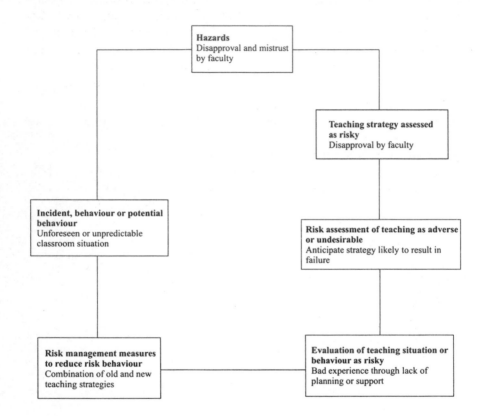

Figure 6.2 Identifying risk in adopting new teaching strategies (adapted from Fox, 1999)

New technologies are transforming teaching and therefore pose a risk, which has to be evaluated, to new teachers. Such evaluation may be based on anecdote or personal experience of problems or evaluations from previous attempts. What does this mean for academics who wish to explore and innovate in their teaching, in environments that perceive such innovations as not the main concern of the academic? It is because of an analysis of risks that the hazard comes into existence? If the risk of introducing new technologies is perceived as zero, then the use of new technologies would not be a problem and the academic would go ahead. There lies the nub of the problem for professional development in terms of teaching, learning and scholarship. If professional development activities encourage academics to engage in new and innovative approaches to teaching and learning within their disciplines, and specifically in terms of considering teaching as scholarship, then how academics perceive these innovations in terms of taking risks within their faculty has significant implications for changing the way teaching, learning and scholarship are viewed and consequently enhanced. Maybe professional development should also include aspects of risk management (see Figure 6.3) to ensure that individual academics take risks in the scholarship of teaching and document their management of the risks they have encountered and the developments they have achieved.

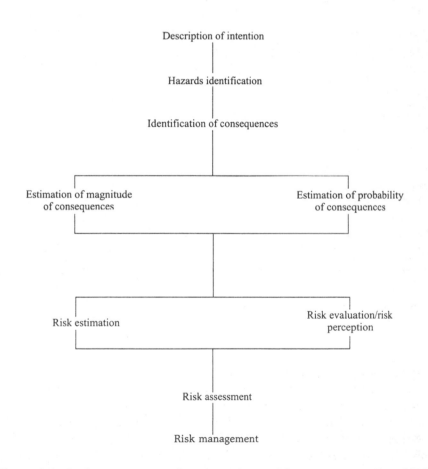

Figure 6.3   Risk management: from intention to risk management (Fox, 1999)

Concluding comments

This chapter has attempted to make connections between scholarship, research, teaching/learning and professional development in the context of higher education. The implications of the connections are used to demonstrate how the development of academic teachers and the reflexive process of learning require understanding that can be gained through professional development activities related to academic disciplines. This type of development allows for the understanding of both pedagogic and knowledge-based issues within given discipline areas to be explored and exemplified. The argument has concentrated on the assumption that if individual academics understand the learning process, teaching will improve and student learning will be enhanced.

With the growing significance and importance of the interrelationship between teaching, learning and research, it is necessary for those involved in teaching in higher education to start thinking about teaching and research as being complementary forms of scholarship. If teaching is going to be more than just a technique and a process by which our understanding of disciplines, or interdisciplinary or professional fields is to be enhanced, then teaching has to be reconnected to scholarship and to the scholarly communities through habits of documentation, exchange and peer review. For this to occur, I have argued that professional development has a strong part to play. It should enable academics to understand and engage in the teaching–learning process. It should also facilitate the development of teaching strategies underpinned by the symbiotic capacity that the scholarship of teaching offers. This then places the role of professional development firmly in the framework of learning and scholarly activity.

In the realms of higher education the status of teaching, both as a professional activity and as a sphere of research, must be raised. This will then highlight and facilitate discussions related to the relationship between teaching, learning and research. One of the most crucial questions needing to be addressed now is: how can teaching help develop research and improve the quality of learning? Elton's statement on the topic of professional development is still valid and possibly even more pertinent today: 'One is left with the impression that staff development in higher education is many faceted and that it is still looking for a sense of direction' (1977: 2).

With the reality of teacher training for university academics being implemented in higher education, now is the time to 'move beyond the tired old "teaching versus research" debate and give the familiar and honourable term "scholarship" a broader, more capacious meaning, one that includes four but interrelated dimensions: discovery, integration, application and teaching' (Boyer, 1990: 1).

7

Ways forward in professional development

Introduction

Chapter 2 considered the implications, demands and functions of the ILT, raising issues related to professionalism and the role of the professional. Chapter 5 extended these arguments, giving us alternative perspectives on how to view the professional academic in both a utopian and realistic context. The discussions suggest that professional development needs new directions and dimensions, which can engage the academic both at an individual level and an institutional level. The terms of engagement must also allow for academics to follow their discipline whilst at the same time beginning to understand the theoretical underpinnings of the pedagogic practice of those disciplines. The present situation and future situations, unless dealt with sympathetically, suggest greater alienation from teaching rather than a greater involvement. Imposed professional development based on operational competence and practical outcomes as set out by the ILT lends itself to abuse. By this I mean that academics can, and will, play the system in order to gain membership. Surely this will lead to a greater crisis in teaching status and effectiveness of practice.

Thus when considering professional development for the future we cannot ignore the possibilities of such crises. These possibilities should be informing the changes that need to take place, and shaping our ideas about learning, research and teaching. The consequence of such shaping should include considering and viewing the relationship of future actions taken in relation to engaging academics in the field of learning, teaching, research and scholarship. Crucial to professional development is understanding how knowledge is viewed in terms of learning, teaching and research.

Throughout the book I have suggested that the changing context of higher education in relation to the increase and diversity of students alongside the expansion and dissemination of knowledge has affected the relationship between learning, teaching and research, as well as the nature of professional development being imposed on higher education. It is now time to allow academics to learn and be learners. For this reason the emphasis in this chapter is on the need to consider professional development as both a personal and a professional learning enterprise. The aim is to show that there are more positive ways forward than imposing a professional development system that is based on operational competence and practical outcomes, which will deter rather than encourage academics to learn and be learners in the field of teaching and learning. We need a system that acknowledges what the role of professional academics is and as such encourages them to develop their knowledge related to teaching and learning in an academic way. This requires the academic to understand the scholarship of teaching. In this way teaching and learning in higher education will necessarily improve.

The discussion revolves around what the central questions related to the future nature of professional development should be and how they should be addressed. If we as a community are trying to raise the status of teaching and learning within the community we must attempt to understand what the issues and central questions are. I would suggest that at this juncture there is one central question that must be asked: *what are the key change factors for academics in higher education and how can professional development facilitate meeting those changes?*

In earlier chapters it has been argued that there is an increasing move towards imposed professional development, a kind of development that ignores the professionality of academics. This point is clearly made in Chapter 5. Much of this lack of understanding of the academics' world has caused discontinuity in their professional development and their ability to learn. What the key factors causing such discontinuity are and how such discontinuity can be averted in the future are the main focus of this chapter.

External regulation

'Regulation is a difficult and emotive concept for academic communities, which value above all other values personal and institutional autonomy (the right of the individual and the institution to decide how to perform their core activities) and academic freedom (the absence of outside interference, censure or obstacles in the pursuit and practice of academic work)' (Jackson, 1998: 5). This statement indicates both the complexities and the comprehensiveness of the concept of regulation. Yet it is a concept that the academic community increasingly has to come to terms with. As Jackson indicates, at the level of the individual it embraces the quality of teaching, and the management and assessment of learning by individual academics working within autonomous or semi-autonomous academic communities. At the level of the institution it embraces a set of activities that encompasses the dimensions of quality management; quality assurance, control and audit; research and inquiry; decision making and the management of public accountability (p 6).

Many of the attempts at reforming teaching and learning in higher education and making it more publicly accountable have been through external regulation. The ILT is a definitive example. Today, such developmental situations are being imposed in circumstances in which initiatives for change at least to some extent are in the hands of higher education institutions. The reforms that are being brought about are aimed to change, improve and develop academic teachers and, through them, teaching. Reforms aimed at improving teaching styles have been unsuccessful, or else methods have been slow in changing. Academics' conceptions of what constitutes good teaching have been deeply rooted (Rowland, 1999), since the beliefs that underlie the conceptions are resistant to change and reinforced through extensive experience. As a consequence, surface changes such as those encouraged by induction courses can't influence them.

What is important here is that we are considering the notion of change, ie requiring academics to change the way they perceive and implement their learning, teaching and teaching style. When thinking about academic change, there are two areas we need to consider: 1) the issue of someone external to the institution (ILT or Government) attempting to change teaching or more accurately academics; 2) the totally different phenomenon of academics' personal growth.

In both areas, change is the key issue. This being the case, it is essential that we consider the conditions of change and the implications for academics and their institutions. Educational change is a complex process and only just beginning to be understood. It is equally important to recognize that research has shown that much of the collective change that has gone on in education seems to have failed. As Fullan laments, 'Most educational change in education seems to fail, and failure means frustration, wasted time, feelings of incompetence and lack of support, and disillusionment' (1982: 63).

The sentiments portrayed by Fullan have long been recognized and understood by those involved in educational development. However, if as academics we are 'to assist in improving the quality of education provided by our institutions', as has been argued by Lonsdale as the purpose of educational development (Cannon and Lonsdale, 1988: 28), then it is imperative that help is given to bring about collective change in our own institutions. Key here is that the type of change we need to bring about impacts on the whole organization and not just on isolated individuals. Institutions should be looking to understand conditions for change and how these may impact on the professional development of both the institution and the individual.

Conditions for change

Those from outside higher education aiming to achieve change should be aware of, and sensitive to, several factors related to the nature and context of professional development:

- The support given to new academics in their schools, faculties or departments is essential for change in teaching and learning to take place.
- Development of experienced and long-standing staff has an influence on the development of new members of staff.
- Visiting and observing other learning environments, followed by discussion of observations made with other colleagues, are essential if change in belief on the practical level is to be achieved.
- Organization that allows academics to reflect on their thinking and actions is required.

Key in professional development for future academics should be an understanding of what initiates change in learning and teaching. For this to happen academics first need to be 'perturbed' in their thinking and actions and second they need to commit themselves to do something about that 'perturbance'. They should also have a vision of what they would like to see in their learning, teaching and teaching sessions.

The suggestion here is that perturbance is an essential facet of changing academics' views of teaching and learning, and as a consequence should play a part in future concepts of professional development. The central meaning of perturbance is taken from Cobb, Wood and Yackel (1990). They state that the crucial point for a teacher to change is 'when she began to realise her current practice might be problematic' (p 132). For this to occur there are three central concepts to consider: cultural environment, perturbance and commitment. Figure 7.1 shows the connection between the three elements required for change to occur.

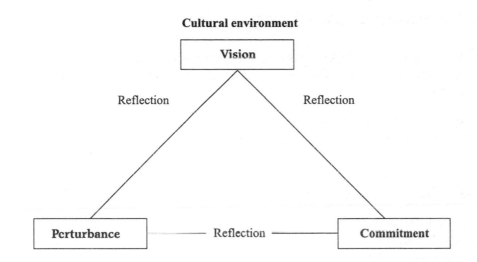

Figure 7.1   The connection between the three elements required for change (adapted from Shaw, Davis and McCarthy, 1991)

Cultural environment

Universities are complex social organizations with distinctive cultures. On the one hand, academic freedom and autonomy are inviolable values and, on the other hand, changing environmental conditions exert strong influences on the primary functions of universities. The ability of a university's cultures to adapt to these changes is questionable. Research suggests that culture influences academic institutions, but it is not clear how university culture functions. The implication is that emphasis can lie on the faculty, the administration, the discipline or the whole organization. What is clear is that universities have unique characteristics that need to be understood and that dominate their culture. In addition to this the culture of universities is often influenced by external elements. As they become more vulnerable to their environment, including changes in political, economic, social and technological conditions, universities have to confront these issues. I would like to argue that the university culture can be a vital element in that confrontation, and that professional development and its role within that culture have a fundamental role to play.

It is accepted here that 'cultural environment' is perceived differently by every academic. I am using a broad definition of university culture here, one that emphasizes the values and beliefs of university members, which are developed in a historical process and transmitted by language or symbols (Deal and Kennedy, 1982).

Within these perceptions, values and beliefs lie some central cultural elements that have impact on the process of change. These include the support given by other academics, time, money, resources, taboos, customs and common beliefs about research, scholarship and teaching. Such elements influence the decision-making strategies of a university (Tierney, 1988). If this is the case, then the culture of the university will play a significant part in the perception, development and implementation of professional development programmes within the institution itself.

The relationship between university culture and strategic management is an element that needs careful and deliberate consideration, if professional development is going to play a major and significant role in the future of the university. Sporn (1996) puts forward a relationship between university culture and strategic management that helps the discussion related to change and professional development. Figure 7.2 shows this relationship.

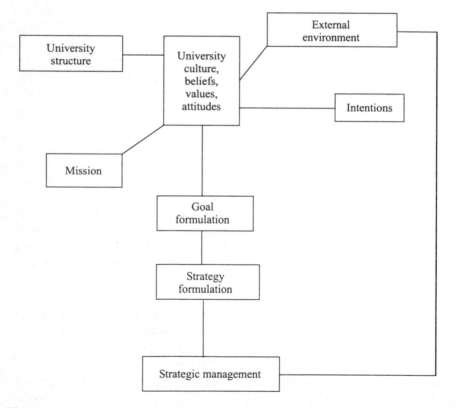

Figure 7.2   Relationship between university culture and strategic management (Sporn 1996)

Although this chapter is not to do with strategic planning *per se*, it is important that we consider the relationship put forward by Sporn in relation to changing the role and perception of professional development within an academic community and university. The above relationship rests on the basic assumption that the university is a complex social organization, which is dependent on the external environment, and that culture plays a major role for strategic management. Sporn argues: 'The specific external environment and the university structure lead to the development of a distinctive academic culture. This culture contains special beliefs, values, and attitudes exhibited by university members' (1996: 47).

The implication of the above-stated relationship for the university and particularly for professional development within universities is the extent of external influence such as the ILT on university culture at the level both of the individual and of the institution as a whole. I would argue that the culture is changing, and the change incurred is increasing the level of conflict between personal and imposed professional development. Tierney (1988) suggests that it is essential to understand university culture as a means of minimizing the occurrence and consequences of cultural conflict and helping foster the development of shared goals. Yet there is little evidence to show that minimizing such conflict is taking place within academic institutions.

By and large the demands of the ILT are being met by imposing training programmes on new individuals to the academy, yet older members of staff established in their ways do not as yet have to have any training themselves. As a consequence they do not understand why such training is required and imposed on new members of staff. Misunderstanding or lack of understanding of this new development initiative often alienates and deters new lecturers from attending such training. This has much to do with the culture of universities, a culture in which older professors have little recent experience of struggling to enter a sluggish or contracting market. As Bennett explains: 'More recent faculty often report an exhausting battle to locate the entry-position that appears to them to have come so easily to their senior colleagues. After years of underemployment and migration among part-time or temporary positions, some newer faculty find their elders simply unable to understand the personal meaning of these vastly changed circumstances' (1999: 9).

The vastly changed circumstances now also include formalized training in learning and teaching. It is interesting to note that these issues with senior staff are not new. Over a decade ago, Boud stated that 'it cannot be denied that the main barrier to the development of more effective professional development programmes is the attitude of the head of department' (1988: 173). Boud goes on to make the point that the Australian Vice-Chancellors' Committee Working Party expressed their reservations about development as follows: 'Heads of departments or schools have a particular responsibility; their apathy or resistance has often been deadly to initiatives in staff development; on the other hand, their discriminating encouragement can change the atmosphere within a department' (1981: viii).

Reconciling these different faculty experiences is difficult and contributes to the conflict found within institutions, which is perpetuated by the notion of what higher education and academic institutions are or want to be. Giddens (1995: 81) suggests that 'on a cultural level', globalization tends to produce cultural diasporas. Communities of taste, habit and belief frequently become detached from place and from the confines of the institution or nation. Diasporic cultural traits are, he says, quite often standardizing, and influenced by cultural commodification. The culture of the ILT as it stands at present can be seen to mirror such a diasporic culture. It is trying to standardize and commodify the professional development of academics, thus stripping individuals of their beliefs and personal development. Maybe we have reached a time for academics and academic institutions to turn the lights of inquiry and research back upon themselves and be open to change, rather than have the change imposed from outside agencies and pressures.

In order for change to occur within higher education and particularly with respect to professional development, the academic self and the academic community need to be considered. A first step to such a consideration requires looking at the notion of perturbance.

Perturbance

Change cannot come without a 'perturbance' in academics' thinking and action. For example, students, colleagues, academic education, self-reflection, academic articles and books can all act as a source of perturbance. Academics in the process of change need to form a personal vision of what it is to teach and learn their discipline within an academic environment. Research shows (Davies, 1993) that, in order to effect a successful and positive change, academics need first to be 'perturbed' in their thinking and actions and second they need to commit themselves to doing something about that 'perturbance'. The central premise of perturbance is that for academics to change, they must begin to realize that their current practice might be problematic. However, the realization of being 'perturbed' can be and often is a difficult concept to understand and come to terms with in higher education, particularly at the present time when the academy has a widespread disposition to behave in certain ways with regard to research, teaching, learning, scholarship and professional development. The relationships of an individual to self, to others, to the community as a whole and to external agencies have a significant effect on the future directions of professional development in higher education.

Why does the individual's relationship with the self, others, the community as a whole and outside agencies impact on future directions for professional development? This question is complex and needs consideration.

The individual

Being part of an academic institution can dispose the individual to isolation, fragmentation of effort and neglect of the common good of the faculty. In order to examine these elements further with respect to professional development and future change, the individual can be considered from a variety of perspectives, including commitment, vision and change in role.

Commitment
This is a personal decision to realize the change as a result of one or more perturbances. Academics in the process of change need to form a personal vision of what their disciplines' teaching and learning should look like in their sessions. They should not accept what is thrown at them or believed to be the norm. To quote a new lecturer's view of how teaching was perceived in the department: 'we have always taught through large lectures and making the students take notes; that is what we expect'. Thus if change is to be experienced in teaching and learning, academics should be positively encouraged to be actively involved in the planning stages of innovations and curriculum developments, rather than be expected to perpetuate old teaching material and teaching styles. Healy (2000) argues that 'developing a scholarly approach to our teaching is, I believe, to link the process explicitly to the disciplines in which we are based'.

Vision
The component of having a personal vision is a powerful but often neglected factor in the formation and development of beliefs, as when we are looking for change it is a personal change. This requires consideration of two fundamental aspects of being an academic, those of change in role and change in viewpoint.

Change in role
In terms of professional development and ways forward, change in role is a prerequisite of a change in learning and teaching. It requires thinking about scholarship, the type of scholarship Greetz (1980) calls 'a fundamental change in the way we think about the way we think'. The change in role constitutes a change in perception by the academics themselves, a change from teacher to learner, or what Boyer calls the scholarship of discovery. This then lets us consider future professional development in terms of change of role, where individual academics are forced to identify themselves as learners, thus making them think about ways in which they

capture their own learning and teaching experience as a means to helping them assess the impact they have on those who are trying to learn from them, as well as assessing their own learning. Such a situation offers academics the opportunity to observe themselves from outside; as a result, 'perturbance' is caused in their thinking, which is a prerequisite for change and development.

Promoting learning

Perturbance is an essential ingredient to activate reflective learning, whether it be on general academic practice, teaching or research. It is therefore important to discuss the concept of reflection within the argument of professional development. Here, Mezirow's three levels of reflection are taken as the starting-point. These three levels relate to content, process and premise. Mezirow argues that:

> one reflects on the content of a problem, or situation when it is described: the questions that should then be asked include 'What did or should I do?' This then leads to descriptions of the problem. We engage in process reflection when we reflect on the strategies we used for problem solving and the suitability of the approaches taken: How did I do it? Were my strategies effective? Might be an example of process reflection. When we become involved in premise reflection we explore 'the merit and functional relevance of the question'.
>
> (Mezirow, 1992: 105)

The reasons Mezirow's three levels are useful to us in the context of future professional development is that they facilitate the consideration that scholarship involves learning and teaching, as both require a demonstration of knowledge of the type Habermas (1974) terms instrumental, communicative and emancipatory. The suggestion here is that learning and eventually knowing about teaching involve all three processes. This also allows for Boyer's different forms of scholarship to be brought together so that knowledge and process guide each form of scholarship.

How then can types of knowledge and process guide a professional development framework?

Here the work of Kreber and Cranton (Kreber, 1999) is useful to explore. They suggest a model for the scholarship of teaching that involves both the learning about teaching and the demonstration of that knowledge. They put forward the premise that there are three different knowledge domains: instructional knowledge, pedagogical knowledge and curricular knowledge. Instructional knowledge refers to the knowledge teachers need to acquire in the area of instructional design, such as knowledge about teaching strategies, sequencing of instruction, formulating learning objectives, constructing tests and so forth. Pedagogical knowledge refers to what we know about how students learn. Pedagogical knowledge informs instructional knowledge. It includes an understanding of learning style, cognitive style, the cognitive and affective processes involved in learning, and group dynamics. Pedagogical knowledge is concerned with how to teach the content of the discipline, how to assist students in problem solving and thinking within the discipline and how to foster thinking and learning beyond the discipline. Curricular knowledge refers to goals, purposes, rationale of course or of larger questions as to why we teach the way we teach (Kreber and Cranton, 1999: 312).

This enables us to consider knowledge from a variety of perspectives. The above three forms can also be regarded as either declarative (knowing that) or procedural (knowing how). In terms of learning and particularly in the workplace it is essential to consider the types of knowledge that are explicit and publicly shared, and knowledge that is tacit or implicit. This is particularly important when thinking of academics, who are constantly learning from their research in their discipline and learning from learning within the academic community, by which is meant the type of knowledge needed or required in order to adapt to a specific environment (such as the unspoken rules that govern the higher education workplace), which is not explicitly taught and indeed often not verbalized. This is particularly the case in higher education in relation to the status of research and teaching (Nicholls, 2000). Sternberg exemplifies this notion by suggesting that knowledge here is not disembodied facts, or even information, but rather is the 'veil through which we see and interpret the world and interact with the world' (1994: 223).

Framework for future professional development

Tony Becher (1996) suggests that an 'academic profession is defined by its concern for learning'. This notion was explored in earlier chapters, which showed how the academic's role has changed and shifted. Whilst the shift, according to Becher, has served to enhance research through the RAE, the emergent change in the 'value' of teaching has diminished and lost prestige. Both these shifts have implications for enhancement of professional skills and modification of professional practice.

In response to these shifts has been the introduction of induction courses in learning and teaching, often emphasizing generic qualities and standardization of the learning environment. There is no doubt that such courses and training programmes are important elements of staff induction and development, but on their own they have only marginal status. Professional development of the academic must not be seen as being synonymous with attendance at courses, particularly when many of these induction courses are happening at work and given by educational developers or fellow academics. Learning in the workplace is seen as an ongoing process, often influenced by the circumstances in which the set activities are engaged with (Billett, 1998: 48). This brings with it many issues, most notably the centrality of learning and the importance of the context in which that learning is taking place and encouraged.

Increasingly the ability to learn is itself regarded as a principal competency, one that distinguishes the successful from the less successful practitioner. This ability to learn is made up of a complex of personal attitudes and abilities, many of which may be enhanced through personal and professional development interventions. However, consideration has to be given to what it means to the academic to learn at work. Garrick suggests:

> When work *is* learning there is clearly a range of critical issues and tensions arising. With the growth of interest in the demand for learning at work, future directions appear to include the need for workplaces to be active in supporting workers/learners as well as deconstructing the limiting conceptual differences between 'workers', 'managers', 'supervisors', and 'educators'. This deconstruction could involve, for example, a surfacing of the effects of the related power imbalances that such distinctions construct.
>
> (Garrick, 1999: 227)

Any future framework of professional development for the academic has to take heed of these words. Although Garrick was describing a scenario for industry, the same principles apply to higher education. Let us consider the implications for supporting the learning of academics within their workplace. Already the ILT requires peer observation and critical review of progress. Often senior members of staff conduct these. Heads of school or departments are also responsible for encouraging and supporting promotion applications. This dual role of senior members of staff puts the academic wishing to learn in the workplace in a difficult position, particularly when learning happens through the engagement of routine and non-routine problem-solving activities influenced by a particular community practice, whether this be the mode of delivery of teaching, conducting of research or the way courses are developed and assessed. Billett states that everyday participation in work tasks provides opportunities for learners to generate tentative solutions to vocational tasks and to attempt to secure those solutions (1998: 48).

Although participation at work does provide learning opportunities it is important to appreciate the anxieties that learning and particularly learning in the workplace brings. Barnett encapsulates this well. He argues:

> Learning itself is unsettling in personal terms. To admit to being a learner is to admit to being uncertain, and in that admission, all too frequently one is in danger of losing one's authority – or one feels that that is the case. This is particularly so if, in that disclosure one opens oneself up to a learning situation in which one has to learn a technique or grasp a set of ideas in part from a junior colleague.
>
> (Barnett, 1999: 35)

Barnett's analysis has a significant bearing on a professional development framework for an academic community that is involved in learning and associated with learning as a central feature of its business.

I believe that learning has to become a central feature of any future framework that takes account of, and is seen to be within the context of, the academic and the community. As Matthews and Candy highlight, 'the ability and potential to go on learning is important, not only for the individual but for the entire organization as well' (1999: 47).

The suggested framework (see Figure 7.3) has three distinct but interrelated elements: professional development programme, new members of staff and head of department or senior member of staff. Each element has an identifiable role, with responsibilities and expectations that are accountable. The framework allows focus to centre on individuals as learners and perceive them as resources, as distinct from the process and networks they are connected to, or associated with.

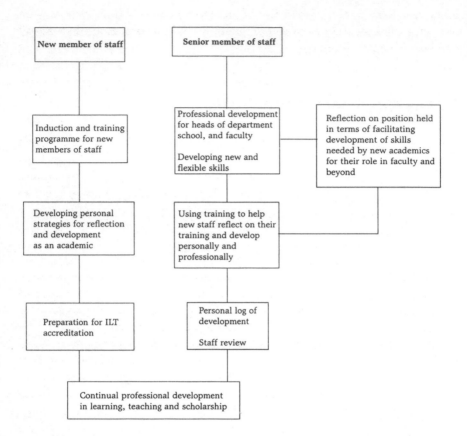

Figure 7.3   Framework for inclusive professional development based on reflective learning

The suggested framework is to be seen as an inclusive process, whereby heads of departments and senior colleagues take an active role in the developmental process. The framework is not seen as a token gesture; it must reflect the institution's responsibility in accepting the challenge of focusing attention on those who are fundamentally responsible – the heads of department, school or faculty, and other senior staff. If a professional development framework does not actively involve heads in how they treat their staff, the impact will be necessarily limited (Moses, 1985). This is a very strong argument and one that must be headed at this moment in time. The ILT expects new members of the academic world to be trained, but not established senior members of staff. But if Moses' argument is to hold, the implication is that training for heads of department, school or faculty, and other senior members of staff should also be initiated. Figure 7.3 illustrates how an inclusive professional development programme could be orchestrated so that all members of faculty develop mutually.

Applying the framework

As we have seen in Chapter 2, the ILT requires evidence related to teaching and learning. This evidence can take a variety of forms, but has to include programme development, peer observation and personal reflection. Accredited programmes and workshops are providing most of these elements at present. However, workshops and development programmes in themselves are insufficient. They are a necessary part of the infrastructure required to support professional development, especially in the area of teaching and learning where most new staff have little or no training or prior experience. It is important to remember that academics are contracted as researchers and teachers and as such require skills in administration and management. Acceptance that academics need these skills to be functional within higher education implies a professional development framework that incorporates or at the very least reflects these needs and demands.

If academics are to identify themselves as learners, they require a professional development framework that addresses issues related to competency and reflective-based learning. Figure 7.3 shows the reflective framework of a development approach. Figure 7.4 shows how a competency approach can also steer professional development. I am not advocating a competency approach, but suggesting that any future professional development frameworks have to be a synergy of a learning model that allows learning to be both reflective and pragmatic.

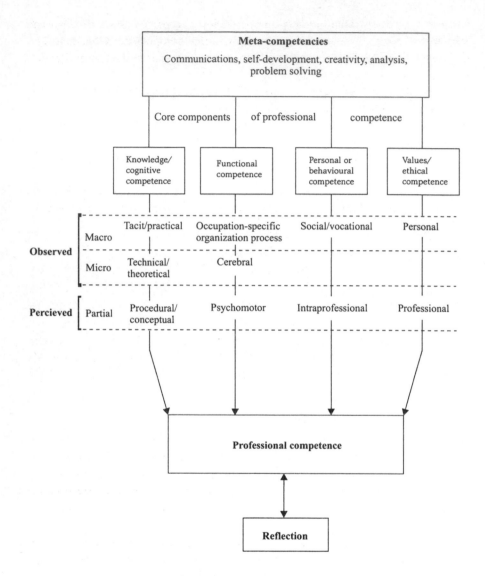

Figure 7.4 Generic professional model (proposed by Cheetham and Chivers, 1996)

Cheetham and Chivers's generic professional model combines a competence-based approach to development with that of the 'reflective practitioner' (Schön, 1983): a combination that reflects the academic community. The model suggests a set of overarching meta-competencies (competencies required for any job) and a set of core components of professional competence. Cheetham and Chivers define each of these core component competences in the following way:

- *knowledge/cognitive competence*: 'possession of appropriate work-related knowledge and the ability to put this to effective use';
- *functional competence*: 'ability to perform a range of work-based tasks effectively to produce a specific outcome';
- *personal or behavioural competence*: 'ability to adopt appropriate behaviours in work-related situations';
- *values/ethical competence*: 'possession of appropriate personal and professional values and the ability to make sound judgements based on these in work-related situations'.

These definitions fit well with our view of professionalism and the nature of the professional role of the academic (see Chapter 5). The model reflects each of the elements required by academics to meet their responsibilities and accountability as members of an academic community. The model acknowledges that academics require a knowledge base, skills and competencies to underpin their teaching, management and administrative duties, as well as that they should be reflective in the learning of their skills and knowledge. Continual reflection, evaluation and development are key to the model. The Cheetham and Chivers model is particularly relevant in conjunction with the suggested inclusive framework of development for the following reasons:

- It allows areas of specific competence appropriate to the main functional role of the academic to be determined. This allows the academic to identify both personal and professional pathways to develop those core requirements. For the new academic it may mean learning about teaching or administration; for the more senior academic it may mean learning new research techniques or financial skills.
- It allows for individual institutional contexts to be taken into account. Here an organization that is predominately teaching-orientated may wish new colleagues to develop research and scholarship skills.
- It facilitates the reflection of certain methodologies, values and norms often associated with specific disciplines to be recognized and given currency.
- It allows for ownership of the conceptual framework for development at the level of department, school and individual.
- It provides a focus for institutional training and induction as well as continual professional development at the level of school, department and individual.

- Its most valuable element is that it allows for both formal and informal methods of evaluation in respect of professional review, and allows individuals to identify their learning at various levels, institutionally, personally and professionally.

A combination of the inclusive framework and the generic professional model exemplifies the need for academics to be self-regulatory and accountable within the academic community.

Concluding remarks

Within the proposed framework and discussion of professional development, learning and work have been central to the argument but have not been taken to be synonymous. They have been explained as different but overlapping concepts. This we have shown is especially the case in higher education, where learning by pushing back the frontiers of knowledge is expected, and indeed often rewarded. Yet, many of the skills and competencies such as teaching, managing and scholarship are taken for granted as being part of work, an element that is rarely connected to learning. There lies the nub of the problem with respect to professional development in higher education. However, the proposed framework allows individuals to learn and be accountable to their institutions. It reflects learning and emphasizes the need for academics to be aware of their learner identity. Considering areas of competence within a reflective, evaluative and learning framework allows academics at whatever stage of their development to continue learning personally and professionally.

8

Beyond the ILT

Teaching is the highest form of understanding.

(Aristotle)

Accepting Aristotle's statement requires the academic community not only to reflect on its own mission statements but to raise fundamental questions relating to the future context and content of professional development in higher education in relation to teaching and learning programmes. Throughout the book, issues have been raised concerning learning, teaching, scholarship, reflection, competence and assessment. Each has a fundamental role to play when the development of the new and of the experienced academic is being considered. Equally the quality of any future professional education programmes will depend on keeping teaching, learning, scholarship and the role of reflection clearly in sight. However, what needs to be made explicit is the nature and context of the outcomes to be assessed, whether a competency-based model, technocratic model or apprenticeship-style model is adopted. What must be kept in mind is the quality of provision, for both professional education and the long-term use of professional education that academics will be engaged in.

Why beyond the ILT?

The concept and inception of the ILT have been a well-meaning and significant attempt to raise the profile and status of teaching and learning within higher education. But in the rapidly changing world of higher education, what are the prospects for the ILT?

The ILT represents an accrediting body that in essence assesses and monitors the development of academics, with specific reference to their abilities or at the

127

very least perceived abilities in the field of teaching and learning. But is this actually possible? Does the climate of completion rates, shrinking funds, increased student numbers and need to keep research ratings up allow for a real and sustained improvement in teaching quality as prescribed by the ILT?

How will institutions maintain standards, even if they are committed to the principles of the ILT? New academics have a great deal of pressure put on them to perform within their disciplines. This usually means gaining research funds, publishing, administering and teaching. Will these increased pressures, in a sector that has most of its staff on short-term or fixed-term contracts, be conducive to raising both the profile and standard of teaching?

Heads of departments see the demands of the ILT as detracting from what their new members of staff should be doing, ie being research-active. They require the demands for recognition for ILT membership to be kept to a minimum, or as slim-line as possible, so that junior members of staff can learn how to be 'real researchers'. What are the implications of these ingrained attitudes for sustained improvement and recognition in teaching and learning? All this sounds and appears very pessimistic. Possibly what is now required is to start thinking in terms of 'beyond the ILT'.

Beyond the ILT

'Beyond the ILT' by implication suggests that there is no longer a place for the ILT, or that the ILT has not yet found its place within the academic community. Whichever of these scenarios applies, we as an academic community have seriously to consider the implications of imposed professional development that is assessed by outcome and certified by membership to a professional body. We can no longer allow developments to happen to us; we must look at our practices and actively try to construct systems that are conducive to enhancing and raising the standards of teaching, learning and scholarship.

The question that must be asked is: how can institutions cultivate an environment that advocates, recognizes and maintains good teaching from its entire staff? This environment should aim to incorporate all its staff, not just the new members of the academy who have been encouraged to obtain entry into the ILT and thus gain recognition for teaching and learning. It is also essential that the environment should be such that new members of staff, having gained their ILT status, do not revert to 'bad' habits and put teaching on the back burner. How do institutions realistically involve their staff in developing teaching and learning strategies? This requires us to consider issues relating to how academics might learn about teaching, learning and scholarship. Rowland asks: 'What kind of processes might take place when they [academics] work together to develop their educational understanding and practice? How might they draw upon their own and each other's disciplinary understandings? What kind of knowledge might be involved? What kind of enquiry or investigation might be involved in generating this knowledge?' (1999: 303).

These questions, he suggests, lead to a major and more important question: 'What kind of pedagogical theory might underlie the process of learning about teaching for academics?' He follows this question with the assertion: 'Unless those who provide such courses can begin to answer this question, it is difficult to see how they are likely to achieve the envisaged development of university teaching. Indeed, overcoming the public perception that university teaching is amateurish demands that the process of developing university teaching be adequately conceptual' (p 303).

Rowland's point is very significant, and one that needs to be addressed by the ILT as well as higher education institutions. This requires thinking about teaching and learning as being more than developing teaching techniques in a generic way. Applying a technocratic or post-technocratic model of professional education, as described in Chapter 3, will also not assist in developing a conceptualization of teaching and learning. What is required is a serious and full debate on ways in which individual academics can engage with the theoretical and pedagogical perspective as related to their discipline. Chew's example of Richard Feynman is a good starting-point.

Teaching and learning courses have to provide participants with opportunities to engage with a variety of perspectives, thus allowing academics to develop a form of critical reflection that engages them from both a disciplinary and interdisciplinary perspective. Barnett (1990: 165) argues that some such form of critical interdisciplinarity should play at least some part in all students' experience of higher education. What is suggested here is that lecturers, like their students, should gain from this critical approach to their own learning.

Key to the whole perspective of critical reflection in this way is that academics come to understand and share their ideas about learning. It is equally important for them to examine their understanding of the nature of learning (drawn from their own discipline) and how this relates to their practice as teachers and learners.

The issues identified so far have significant implications for the future construction of professional development courses related to teaching and learning. These courses cannot remain, as they often are now, piecemeal and outcome-led. The ILT does not appear to be engaged with this type of dialogue. It is for this reason that higher education institutions need to think 'beyond the ILT', and construct learning frameworks that enable academics to engage with the conceptualization of learning from within their own disciplines and through interdisciplinarity.

A more constructive and purposeful approach to learning is required if academics are to change the perceptions of teaching and learning in higher education. The types of change required will not automatically occur through imposed professional development. What is now needed is for higher education to seize the moment, look beyond what we have now and devise systems that allow personal and professional development to occur, reflecting the accountability of academics to their profession, as well as the goals and values of higher education.

Boyer's plea is for a 'more inclusive view of what it means to be a scholar – a recognition that knowledge is acquired through research, through synthesis, through practice, and through teaching must be a way of unifying research and teaching through the notion of scholarship', a term with 'a broader, more capacious meaning, one that brings legitimacy to the full scope of academic work' (1990: 24). If this is allowed to happen we need to move 'beyond the ILT' and thus move the academic community 'beyond the tired old "teaching versus research" debate' (Boyer, 1990: 16). To do this we need to reconceptualize the universities' core mission around learning (Bowden and Marton, 1998), accepting Boyer's paradigm of scholarship. If this is accepted it may then be possible to create a more relevant, non-hierarchical relationship between the activities of teaching, learning and research. Learning is the key link between research and teaching, and benefits both activities to the mutual advantage of both teacher and learner (Moses, 1990; Rowland, 1996).

For the higher education community to go beyond the ILT it needs to take stock of how it is to provide and more importantly support professional development in respect to teaching and learning for both the individual and the institution. For this type of discussion to happen I would suggest that the role of the academic be considered from two perspectives, that of the learning-based professional and that of the discipline-based professional.

The learning-based professional

Boyer reminds us: 'Great teachers create a common ground of intellectual commitment. They stimulate active, not passive, learning and encourage students to be critical, creative thinkers with the capacity to go on learning' (1990: 13).

This statement refers not just to lecturers teaching their students, but to the lecturers themselves. Academics have to become learners and acknowledge the fact that they are learning all the time, and that part of being a professional is that one is actively engaged in that learning. Professional learning that accepts and acknowledges the application and utilization of knowledge is the key to good professional development. The individual role within that learning also has to be acknowledged and made accountable.

If we are positioning professional development within a learning framework, and that the framework is essential for individuals to be able to demonstrate their learning, mechanisms for reviewing the development have to be in place. The nature of the review will reflect all elements of the 'professional role'. Chapter 4 addressed the issues of assessment, suggesting that certain areas within the academic's role could be assessed. These were represented as shown in Figure 8.1.

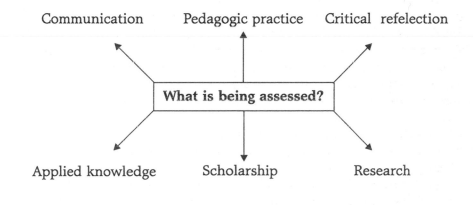

Communication   Pedagogic practice   Critical refelection

What is being assessed?

Applied knowledge   Scholarship   Research

Figure 8.1 Areas of assessment

Through the discussion it has become apparent that the present assessment is based on an operational competence model that looks for evidence primarily related to practical outcomes in relation to teaching and learning design. Of the areas of assessment shown in Figure 8.1, we can say that no more then two are currently being assessed by the ILT, those of pedagogic practice and possibly critical reflection. Although I have argued that the type of reflection that should be demanded is the one of critical reflection, the ILT's demands tend to make academics reflect in operational mode rather than academic mode. Thus individuals involved in the assessment procedure are unlikely to be learning in a deep way. Rather, they are involved in surface learning, by being asked to reflect on pedagogic practice in a superficial way, which is concerned with changing operational and mechanistic elements of their teaching, rather than with the important aspects of why students did or did not engage in learning, or how one makes students understand certain concepts. Evidence related to this type of reflection requires individuals to learn and be prepared to learn about learning and learning environments. I have emphasized the notion of academics recognizing that they too are learners; it would therefore be appropriate that academics demonstrate their learning, and that learning should become central to their development. Figure 8.1 might then be redrawn by placing learning at the centre and thereby relating all areas of the academic's role to learning. This is shown in Figure 8.2. In this way there is an acceptance that learning about teaching is as important as learning through research.

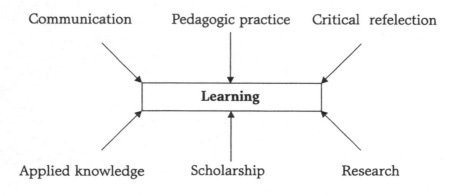

Figure 8.2   Learning at the centre of professional development

When learning, rather than assessment, is placed at the centre of professional development, it allows us to look at how academics may plan their development, from both a personal and an institutional perspective. It is therefore equally important to position the other aspect of academics' professional development, that of their commitment to their discipline.

The discipline-based professional

Much of the discussion so far has related to academics being associated with and aligned to a type of professionalism directly attributed to their discipline. It has also been suggested that for this purpose members of the academic community have been at odds with the demands of the ILT, especially in relation to professional development. Yet the ILT has a claim to being a professional body for academics involved in teaching and learning support. If academics are to be recognized as professionals and as such accountable for their actions as teachers in the higher education community, then there must be a mechanism in place both to demonstrate that professionality and to show how that professionality is accountable. After all, reference to a profession is usually positive, imputing status and prestige, denoting a desirable form of work, which is accomplished with competence. For these reasons, many occupational groups claim the title in their struggles for social position and approval. Yet this does not seem to be the case with academics and the ILT. The exact nature of the professionalism offered by the ILT is unclear and as such is being rejected by many in the academic community. A possible reason for this is that academics in higher education have a large amount of autonomy and individualism, and no constant and exacting peer review of their teaching and learning. As has been discussed previously, academics need to preserve this autonomy, and as a consequence have rejected the imposition of the ILT, not the principles of a professional body.

Higher education and the academics within it do require autonomy in the exercise of expertise, but autonomy needs to be counterbalanced by clear structures of public accountability. The dilemma that is before the higher education community is that the present structures of the ILT are not clear enough; they are too prescriptive and too generic in outcome, thus leaving the impression that all academics need to conform to a particular protocol.

This being the case, the higher education community needs to look for an alternative structure or accountability system that shows publicly and effectively that teaching and learning support are part of their professional role. The notion of accountability will not disappear. If we return to what a professional body is for and the nature of professionalism called for by a professional body, then we have to remind ourselves that professionalism means a service to our clientele, and that the good of that clientele is paramount and reviewed regularly.

At present the standing of the higher education community in respect to teaching and learning is not assured. Accordingly, academics need to think carefully before they claim their uncontested right as professionals in the field of teaching and learning support. For professional academics within a discipline, their claim is to specialized knowledge rather than a knowledge or expertise related to the communication of that specialized knowledge. Academics within a field are not known for formal or informal discussions related to teaching, learning and how to relate their intellectual inquiry to student learning needs. Unlike those in other professional groups, much of the academic community spends little collective time or energy reviewing ways to improve teaching, learning and support service to students. If efforts to change teaching and improve learning through professional development activities are to succeed, the higher education community will need to look closely at its institutional values, rewards and behaviours.

An alternative approach for future professional development

What is required is an alternative perspective or model that relates professional development to ways in which academics can develop through self-critical and peer review. One such model is that put forward by Bennett (1999) based on relationality within the academic community as a means of describing professionalism. This model allows the professionalism of the academic to be viewed differently, with alternative parameters being set up to make that professionalism accountable. Bennett's model holds that the full exercise of higher-order intellectual skills demands engagement with students, colleagues and the broader public. It is only in application in teaching and service that intellect is completed and fulfilled, thereby meeting the other criteria of professionalism: those of value to society and expert knowledge (p 40). As Bennett suggests: 'Informed by the relational model the academy is better able to regulate itself. The hospitality and thoughtfulness that are marks of the relational model and the collegial ethic, push individual faculty towards greater openness to others and to common good. The case for our status as professionals is much stronger when presented through the relational model' (p 44).

However, this type of relational model has rarely enjoyed the dominant influence in academic or disciplinary professionalism. Academics have tended to concentrate their attention inwards, in a way that characterizes the deeply entrenched professionalism of traditional academic disciplines. This has been the case for a considerable time and increasingly, with the threat of imposed generic professional development demands, that entrenchment has become more steadfast. Hence with the imposed demands of the ILT, professionalism within the academic community has continued to define itself as disciplinary professionalism. The consequence of this definition is that one can argue that each academic discipline, not higher education, constitutes a profession. The evidence for this is that we have professors of history, chemistry and psychology, not just professors, and it is research, not teaching, that provides the expertise that qualifies one as a professor. Thus disciplines are identified as professions, and established hierarchies of status among members define intellectual legitimacy and prestige.

It is not surprising that the ILT has taken such a prescriptive view to teaching, learning and professional development. This is not to condone the ILT. It is merely to raise awareness of how perceptions of academic activity can lead to inaccurate or inappropriate forms of accountability. If the higher education community is to have public accountability, there is no doubt that some form of credible evidence related to all aspects of professional conduct within the academic community is required.

The relational model would involve critical self-review of individuals irrespective of rank or position held within the faculty. The process would be seen as part and parcel of the development of the faculty. Evidence from these reviews would be taken to staff development reviews/appraisal for negotiating further development as appropriate to individuals. Formalizing such a process would raise the status of teaching among the academic community, as the venture would be recognized as relational, not individualistic and mechanistic. Such a model lends itself well to a learning-based professional development programme.

Concluding comments

Much has been said about imposed professional development, regulation and intervention in professional practice within the higher education sector. Introducing a professional body for learning and teaching in higher education has generated significant political interest as well as academic consternation at the nature, context and implications of such a body. The arguments related to the purpose, position and authority of the ILT have in many ways detracted from the original purpose for its creation in the first instance. Its core function was to raise the status of teaching and learning in higher education, and provide pathways for achieving this.

An alternative view can be taken regarding these changes. Pennington describes the situation by suggesting: 'A more accurate and less alarmist view would be that the establishment of a national framework for higher education teaching represents a drawing together of many elements which have arisen from good practice within the sector itself over at least two decades of evolutionary change' (1999: 15). This may well be the case, but one cannot ignore the way in which the national framework has been imposed. It has been accepted that the academic community must consider its fundamental values and behaviours if real change is to take place and teaching and learning are to be rewarded within faculty. Encouraging systematic professional development is crucial, if knowledge and skills are to be kept up to date and effective. Developing teaching competence is an aim that is shared, in principle, by all higher education institutions. What is missing is the delivery of this aim, which requires recognition of the time and effort needed by an individual to reach a demonstrable level of operational and academic competence.

Effective professional development must reflect the values of higher education if academics are to engage in a way that will facilitate learning and encourage critical reflection. Professional development activities of the future will only be successful if the national framework is structured but flexible, and encourages personal growth and development rather than prescriptive, generic values and assessment. Enhancement of learning and the development of conceptual tools are key to the lifelong learner. Self-critical review is one way of achieving this. As many in higher education already know and understand, self-review, self-regulation and professional autonomy flourish only where there is confidence in academic communities' responsibility to their learners and to their own learning.

References and further reading

References

Accreditation and Teaching in Higher Education Planning Group (1998) Booth Report, www.cvcp.ac.uk

Ainley, P (1994) *Degrees of Difference: Higher education in the 1990s*, Lawrence and Wishart, London

Australian Vice-Chancellors' Committee (1981) Academic staff development: report of AVCC Working Party, *Occasional Paper No 4*, Vice Chancellors' Committee, Canberra, Australia

Baptiste, I (1999) Beyond lifelong learning: a call to civically responsible change, *International Journal of Lifelong Education*, **18** (2), pp 94–102, March–April

Barnett, R (1990) *The Idea of Higher Education*, SRHE/Open University Press, Buckingham

Barnett, R (1994) *The Limits of Competence: Knowledge, higher education and society*, SRHE/Open University Press, Buckingham

Barnett, R (1997) *Higher Education: A critical business*, SRHE/Open University Press, Buckingham

Barnett, R (1999) Learning to work and working to learn, in *Understanding Learning at Work*, ed D Boud and J Garrick, Routledge, London

Barnett, R (2000) *Realizing the University in an Age of Supercomplexity*, SRHE/Open University Press, Buckingham

Bass, R (1999) The scholarship of teaching: what's the problem?, *Inventio*, **VI** (1), http://www.doiiit.gmu.edu/Archives/feb98/rbass.htm

Becher, T (1989) *Academic Tribes and Territories*, SRHE/Open University Press, Buckingham

Becher, T (1994) The state and the university curriculum in Britain, *European Journal of Education*, **29** (3), pp 231–45

Becher, T (1996) The learning professions, *Studies in Higher Education*, **21** (1), pp 43–56

Bennett, J (1999) *Collegial Professionalism: The academy, individualism, and the common good*, American Council on Education, Oryx Press, Washington

Berliner, D (ed) (1996) *Handbook of Educational Psychology*, Macmillan, New York

Biggs, J B (1996) Enhancing teaching through constructive alignment, *Higher Education*, 32, pp 1–18

Billett, S (1998) Understanding workplace learning: cognitive and sociocultural perspectives, in *Current Issues and New Agendas in Workplace Learning*, ed D Boud, pp 47–68, National Centre for Vocational Education Research, Adelaide

Bolam, R (1987) Conceptualising in service, in *In-Service Training and Educational Development: An international survey*, ed D Hopkins, Croom-Helm, Beckenham

Bottery, M and Wright, N (1996) Cooperating in their own deprofessionalisation? On the need to recognise the 'public' and 'ecological' roles of the teaching profession, *British Journal of Educational Studies*, **44** (1), pp 82–98

Bottery, M and Wright, N (1997) Impoverishing a sense of professionalism: who's to blame?, *Educational Management and Administration*, **25** (1), pp 7–25

Boud, D (1988) Professional development and accountability: working with newly appointed staff to foster quality, *Studies in Higher Education*, **13** (2), pp 165–76

Boud, D, Keogh, R and Walker, D (ed) (1985) *Reflection: Turning experience into learning*, Kogan Page, London

Bowden, J and Marton, F (1998) *The University of Learning: Beyond quality and competence in higher education*, Kogan Page, London

Boyatzis, R E, Cowan, S S and Knolb, D A (1995) *Innovation in Professional Education*, Jossey-Bass, San Francisco, CA

Boyer, E (1987) *College: The undergraduate experience in America*, Harper and Row, New York

Boyer, E (1990) *Scholarship Reconsidered: Priorities of the professional*, Carnegie Foundation for the Advancement of Teaching, Princeton, NJ

Brew, A (1999) Research and teaching: changing relationships in a changing context, *Studies in Higher Education*, **23** (3), pp 291–301

Brew, A and Wright, T (1990) Changing teaching styles, *Distance Education*, **11**, pp 183–212

Brockbank, M and McGill, J (1998) *Facilitating Reflective Learning in Higher Education*, SRHE/Open University Press, Buckingham

Brookfield, S D (1991) *Developing Critical Thinkers*, Open University Press, Milton Keynes

Brynmor Jones Report (1965) *Report of the Committee on Audio-Visual Aids in Higher Education*, HMSO, London

Buchbinder, H and Rajagopal, P (1995) Canadian universities and the impact of austerity on the academic workplace, in *Academic Work: The changing labour process in higher education*, ed J Smyth, pp 60–73, SRHE/Open University Press, Buckingham

Burnard, P (1995) *Learning Human Skills: An experiential and reflective guide for nurses*, 3rd edn, Butterworth/Heinemann, Oxford

Bruner, J S (1985, first published 1966) *Toward a Theory of Instruction*, Harvard University Press, Cambridge, MA

Candy, P C (1994) *Self-direction for Life Long Learning: A comprehensive guide to theory and practice*, Jossey-Bass, San Francisco

Cannon, R A and Lonsdale, A J (1988) A 'muddled array of models': theoretical and organisational perspectives on change and development in higher education, *Higher Education*, **16** (1), pp 21–32

Carnegie Foundation (1999) Scholarship of teaching and learning framework, http://www.carnegiefoundation.org/CASTL/highered/docs/scholars.htm

Cheetham, G and Chivers, G (1996) Towards a holistic model of professional competence, *Journal of European Industrial Training*, **20** (5), pp 20–30

Chew, S (2000) *Teaching and Scholarship: The case of Richard Feynman*, The American Association of Higher Education, New Orleans

Cobb, P, Wood, T and Yackel, E (1990) Classrooms as learning environments for teachers and researchers, in *Constructivist Views on the Teaching and Learning of Mathematics*, JRME Monograph No 4, ed R B Davis, C A Maher and N Noddings, pp 125–46, NCTM, Reston, VA

Damrosch, D (1995) *We Scholars: Changing the culture of the university*, Harvard University Press, Cambridge, MA

Davies, G (1993) Meeting the needs of the society it serves: an industrialist's perception, *Education and Training*, **35** (5), pp 17–24

Day, C (1999) *Developing Teachers*, Falmer, London

Deal, E and Kennedy, A (1982) *Corporate Culture: The rites and rituals of corporate life*, Addison-Wesley, Reading

Dean, A (1996) *Professional Development in Schools*, Open University Press, Buckingham

Department for Education and Employment (DfEE) (1998) *Higher Education for the 21st Century*, HMSO, London

DfEE (1999) *Implementing the Vision*, HMSO, London

Dewey, J (1933) *How We Think*, Regency, Chicago

Duderstadt, J J (2000) *A University for the 21st Century*, The Michigan University Press, Michigan

Dummett, M (1994) Too many cooks and a capitalist flavour, *Tablet*, Educational Supplement No 71, 8 October, pp 1268–69

Dworkin, R (1996) We need a new interpretation of academic freedom, in *The Future of Academic Freedom*, ed L Menand, The University of Chicago Press, Chicago and London

Edgerton, R, Hutchings, P and Quinlan, K (1991) *The Teaching Portfolio: Capturing the scholarship in teaching*, American Association of Higher Education, Washington

Edwards, R (1997) *Changing Places?*, Routledge, London

Elton, L (1977) Introduction, in *Staff Development in Higher Education*, ed R B Elton and K Simmonds, pp 1–2, Society for Research into Higher Education, Guildford

Elton, L (1986) Research and teaching: symbolism or conflict, *Higher Education*, **15**, pp 299–304

Elton, L (1992) Research, teaching and scholarship in an expanding higher education system, *Higher Education Quarterly*, **46**, pp 252–67

Entwistle, N (1992) *The Impact of Teaching on Learning Outcomes in Higher Education: A literature review*, Committee of Vice-Chancellors and Principals, Universities' and Colleges' Staff Development Agency, Sheffield

Entwistle, N (1997) Introduction: phenomenography in higher education, *Higher Education Research and Development*, **16**, pp 127–34

Entwistle, N (1998) Priorities in research into learning and teaching in higher education, SRHE/CVCP seminar, http://www.srhe.ac.uk/cvcp982.htm

Eraut, M (1994) *Developing Professional Knowledge and Competence*, Falmer, London

Eraut, M (1995) Schön shock: a case for reframing reflection-in-action, *Teachers and Teaching*, **1**, pp 9–22

Evans, G (1991) Lessons in cognitive demands and student processing in upper secondary mathematics, in *Learning and Teaching Cognitive Skills*, ed G Evans, Australian Council for Educational Research, Melbourne

Evans, L and Abbott, I (1998) *Teaching and Learning in Higher Education*, Cassell, London and New York

Feynman, R P, Leighton, R B and Sands, M (1963) *The Feynman Lectures on Physics*, Addison-Wesley, Reading, MA

Fox, K (1999) Postmodern reflections on 'risks', hazards and life choices, in *Risk and Sociocultural Theory*, ed D Lupton, Cambridge University Press, Cambridge

Freidson, E (1994) *Professionalism Reborn*, Polity Press, Cambridge

Fullan, M (1982) *The Meaning of Educational Change*, Teacher College Press, New York

Gamson, Z F (1998) The stratification of the academy, in *Chalk Lines: The politics of work in the managed university*, ed R Martin, pp 103–09, Duke University Press, London

Garrett, V with Bowles, C (1997) Teaching as a profession: the role of professional development, in *Managing Continual Professional Development in School*, ed H Tondinson, Paul Chapman, London

Garrick, J (1999) The dominant discourses of learning at work, in *Understanding Learning at Work*, ed D Boud and J Garrick, Routledge, London

Gibbs, G (1998) Strategic priorities for research into learning and teaching and the role of the Institute for Learning and Teaching, SRHE/CVCP seminar, http://www.srhe.ac.uk/cvcp985.htm

Giddens, A (1995) *Beyond Left and Right*, Polity Press, Cambridge

Gleick, J (1992) *Genius: The life and science of Richard Feynman*, Pantheon, New York

Glew, G (1992) Research and the quality of degree teaching – with specific reference to consumer and leisure studies degree course, CNAA Project Report 38, October, CNAA

Goodstein, D L and Neugebauer, G (1989) in the special preface to *The Commemorative Issue of the Feynman Lectures on Physics*, Addison-Wesley, New York

Greeno, J G (1989) Situations, mental models and generative knowledge, in *Complex Information Processing: The impact of Herbet A Simon*, ed D Klahr and K Kotovsky, Erlbaum Associates, Hillside, NJ

Greetz, C (1980) Blurred genres: the refiguration of social thought, *American Scholar*, Spring

Haberman, J (1989) The idea of the university: learning processes, in *The New Conservatism*, ed J Haberman, Polity Press, Cambridge

Habermas, J (1974) *Knowledge and Human Interest*, Heinemann, London

Hale Report (1964) *Report of the Committee on University Teaching Methods*, HMSO, London

Halsey, A H (1992a) *Opening Wide the Doors of Higher Education*, NCE Briefing No 6, National Commission on Education, London

Halsey, A H (1992b) *The Decline of Donnish Dominion*, Oxford University Press, Oxford

Halsey, A H (1995) Opening wide the doors of higher education, NCE Briefing No 6, National Commission on Education, London

Halton, N and Smith, D (1995) Reflection in teacher education: towards definition and implementation, *Teacher and Teacher Education*, **2**, pp 33–51

Hamilton, A H (1998) *Zealotry and Academic Freedom: A legal and historical perspective*, Transaction Publishers, New Brunswick and London

Hattie, J and Marsh, H W (1996) The relationship between research and teaching: a meta analysis, *Review of Educational Research*, **66**, pp 507–42

Haworth, A (1998) *Free Speech*, Routledge, London

Healy, M (2000) Teaching through the disciplines, *The Times Higher Education Supplement*, London

Horn, M (1999) *Academic Freedom in Canada: A history*, University of Toronto Press, Toronto, Buffalo, London

Huber, M (1999) *Disciplinary Styles in the Scholarship of Teaching: Reflection on the Carnegie Academy for the scholarship of teaching and learning*, http://www.carnegiefoundation.org

Huberman, M (1995) Professional careers and professional development: some implications, in *Professional Development in Education*, ed T R Guskey and H Huberman, Teacher College Press, New York

Jackson, N (1998) Academic regulation in UK higher education, Part III – the idea of 'partnership in trust', *Quality Assurance in Education*, **6** (1), pp 5–18

Jacoby, R (1997) Intellectuals: inside and outside the academy, in *The Postmodern University? Contested visions of higher education in society*, ed A Smith and F Webster, pp 61–71, SRHE/Open University Press, Buckingham

Jarvis, P (1986) *Professional Education*, Croom Helm, London

Jarvis, P (1992) *Paradoxes of Learning*, Jossey-Bass, San Francisco, CA, London

Jarvis, P (1996) Public recognition of lifetime learning, *Lifelong Education in Europe*, **1** (1), pp 10–17

Jarvis, P (1999) *The Practitioner-Researcher: Developing theory from practice*, Jossey-Bass, San Francisco, CA

Jencks, C and Riesman, D (1968) *The Academic Revolution*, Doubleday, New York

Johnson, N (1994) Dons in decline, *Twentieth Century British History*, **5**, pp 370–85

Kant, I (1798, 1979) *The Conflict of the Faculties*, tr M J Gregor, Abaris Books, New York

Knowles, M S (1984) *The Adult Learner: A neglected species*, 3rd edn, Gulf, Houston

Kogan, M, Moses, I and El-Khawas, E (1994) *Staffing Higher Education: Meeting new challenges*, Jessica Kingsley Publishers, London

Kolb, D (1976) *Learning Style Inventory: Technical manual*, McBar, Boston

Kolb, D (1984) *Experiential Learning: Experience as a source of learning*, Prentice Hall, Englewood Cliffs, NJ

Kreber, C (1999) A course-based approach to the development of teaching-scholarship: a case study, *Teaching in Higher Education*, **4** (3), pp 309–25

Layton, D (1968) *University Teaching in Transition*, Oliver Boyd, London

Lortie, D (1975) *Schoolteacher: A sociological study*, Chicago University Press, Chicago, IL

Lynton, E A and Elman, P (1987) *New Priorities for the University*, Jossey-Bass, San Francisco, CA

Marsick, V J and Watkins, K (1990) *Informal and Incidental Learning in the Work Place*, Routledge, New York

Martin, E (1999) *Changing Academic Work: Developing the learning university*, SRHE/Open University Press, Buckingham

Mathews, T H (1963) quoted by Sir Douglas Logan in *Universities: The Years of Challenge*, The Rede Lecture 1963, p 28, Cambridge University Press, Cambridge

Matthews, J H and Candy, P C (1999) New dimensions in the dynamics of learning and knowledge, in *Understanding Learning at Work*, ed J Boud and S Garrick, Routledge, London

McNamara, D (1990) Research on teachers' thinking: its contribution to educating student teachers to think critically, *Journal of Education for Training*, **16** (2), pp 147–60

McNay, I (1998) The Research Assessment Exercise (RAE) and after: 'you never know how it will turn out', *Perspectives: Policy and practice in higher education*, **2** (1), pp 19–22

Menand, L (1996) The limits of academic freedom, in *The Future of Academic Freedom*, ed L Menand, The University of Chicago Press, Chicago and London

Merriam, S B and Caffarella, R S (1991) *Learning in Adulthood: A comprehensive guide*, Jossey-Bass, San Francisco, CA

Mezirow, J (1992) *Transformative Dimensions of Adult Learning*, Jossey-Bass, San Francisco, CA

Miller, H (1995) States, economies and the changing labour processes of academics: Australia, Canada and the United Kingdom, in *Academic Work: The changing labour process in higher education*, ed J Smyth, pp 129–43, SRHE/Open University Press, Buckingham

Moll, L (1990) *Vygotsky and Education: Instruction implications of socio-historical psychology*, Cambridge University Press, New York

Moses, I (1985) The role of the head of department in the pursuit of excellence, *Higher Education*, **14**, pp 337–54

Moses, I (1990) Teaching, research and scholarship in different disciplines, *Higher Education*, **19** (3), pp 351–75

National Commission on Education (1993) *Learning to Succeed*, Report of the Paul Hamlyn Foundation National Commission on Education, Heinemann, London

National Committee of Inquiry into Higher Education (NCIHE) (1997) *Higher Education for a Learning Society* (The Dearing Report), HMSO, London

Neumann, R (1993) Research and scholarship: perceptions of senior administrator, *Higher Education*, **25**, pp 97–110

Newson, J and Buchbinder, H (1988) *The University Means Business*, Garamond Press, Toronto

Nicholls, G (1997) *Collaborative Change in Education*, Kogan Page, London

Nicholls, G (2000) Professional development, research and teaching: implications for new lecturers, *International Journal for Lifelong Learning*, **19** (1)

Nixon, J (1996) Professional identity and the restructuring of higher education, *Studies in Higher Education*, **21** (1), pp 5–16

Nixon, J (1997) Regenerating professionalism within the academic workplace, in *The End of the Professions? The restructuring of professional work*, ed J Broadbent, M Dietrich and J Roberts, pp 86–103, Routledge, London

Nixon, J (1999) Teachers, writers and professionals: is there anybody out there?, *British Journal of Sociology of Education*, **20** (2), pp 207–21

Nixon, J and Ranson, S (1997) Theorising 'agreement': the bases of a new professional ethic, *Discourse: Studies in the cultural politics of education*, **18** (2), pp 197–214

Nixon, J *et al* (1997) Towards a learning profession: changing codes of occupational practice within the 'new' management of education, *British Journal of Sociology of Education*, **21** (1), pp 5–28

Opacic, S (1994) The student learning experience in the mid-1990s, in *The Student Experience*, ed S Haselgrove, pp 157–68, SRHE/Open University Press, Buckingham

Ozga, J (1995) Deskilling a profession: professionalism, deprofessionalisation and the new managerialism, in *Managing Teachers as Professionals in Schools*, ed H Busher and R Saran, pp 21–37, Kogan Page, London

Parry Report (1967) *Report of the Committee on University Teaching*, HMSO, London

Parry, G (1995) England, Wales and Northern Ireland, in *Adults in Higher Education: International perspectives on access and participation*, ed P Davies, pp 102–33, Jessica Kingsley Publishers, London

Parsons, T (1968) The professions, in *The International Encyclopaedia of the Social Sciences*, Macmillan, New York

Pennington, G (1999) Towards a New Professionalism, in *A Handbook for Teaching and Learning in Higher Education*, Fry et al, Kogan Page, London

Perkin, H (1989) *The Rise of Professional Society: England since 1880*, Routledge, London

Piper, D W (1994) *Are Professors Professional?*, Jessica Kingsley Publishers, London

Prosser, M and Trigwell, K (1999) *Understanding Learning and Teaching: The experience in higher education*, SRHE/Open University Press, Buckingham

Randall, J (2000) A profession for the new millennium?, in *Higher Education Re-Formed*, ed P Scott, Falmer Press, London and New York

Rhoades, G and Slaughter, S (1998) Academic capitalism, managed professionals, and supply-side higher education, in *Chalk Lines: The politics of work in the managed university*, ed R Martin, pp 33–68, Duke University Press, London

Rice, E (1992) Towards a broader conception of scholarship: the American context, in *Research and Higher Education*, ed T Winston and R Geiger, SRHE/Open University Press, Buckingham

Robbins Report (1963) *Higher Education*, Report of the committee appointed by the prime minister under the chairmanship of Lord Robbins, 1961–63, Cmnd 2154, HMSO, London

Rorty, R (1996) Does academic freedom have philosophical presuppositions?, in *The Future of Academic Freedom*, ed L Menand, The University of Chicago Press, Chicago and London

Rowland, S (1996) Relationships between teaching and research, *Teaching in Higher Education*, 1 (1), pp 7–20

Rowland, S (1999) The role of theory in a pedagogical model for lecturers in higher education, *Studies in Higher Education*, 24 (3), pp 303–14

Rowland, S et al (1998) Turning academics into teachers?, *Teaching in Higher Education*, 3 (2), pp 133–41

Ryan, A (1999) The American way, *Prospect: Politics, essays, argument*, 44, August/September, pp 24–28

Ryle, G (1944) *The Concept of Mind*, Hutchinson, London

Said, E (1994) *Representations of the Intellectual* (The 1993 Reith Lectures), Vintage, London

Said, E (1996) Identity, authority, and freedom: the potentate and the traveller, in *The Future of Academic Freedom*, ed L Menand, The University of Chicago Press, Chicago and London

Schön, D (1983) *The Reflective Practitioner*, Temple Smith, London

Schön, D (1987) *Educating the Reflective Practitioner*, 1st edn, Jossey-Bass, San Francisco, CA

Schön, D (1989) *Educating the Reflective Practitioner*, 2nd edn, Jossey-Bass, San Francisco, CA

Schwab, J (1964) The practical: a language for the curriculum, *School Review*, 78, pp 1–23

Segal Quince Wicksteed Limited (1996) Selective allocation of research funds, Report to the Higher Education Funding Council for England, June, Segal Quince Wicksteed Limited, Economic and Management Consultants, Cambridge and Edinburgh

Shaw, K L, Davis, N T and McCarthy, J (1991) A cognitive framework for teacher change, *Proceedings of PME-NB*, 13 (2), ed R G Underhill, pp 161–67, Virginia Tech, Blacksburg, VA

Shulman, L S (1987) Knowledge and teaching: foundations of the New Reform, *Harvard Educational Review*, 57 (1), pp 1–22

Shulman, L S (1993) Teaching as community property: putting an end to pedagogical solitude, *Change*, 25 (6), pp 6–7

Shulman, L S (1999) Taking learning seriously, *Change*, July/August, pp 11–17

Shumar, W (1997) *College for Sale: A critique of the commodification of higher education*, Falmer Press, London and Washington, DC

Siegrist, H (1994) The professions, State and Government in theory and history, in *Government and Professional Education*, ed T Becher, SRHE/Open University Press, Buckingham

Smeby, J (1998) Knowledge transmission: the interaction between research and teaching at university, *Teaching in Higher Education*, **3** (1), pp 5–20

Smyth, J (ed) (1995) *Academic Work: The changing labour process in higher education*, SRHE/Open University Press, Buckingham

Sporn, D (1996) Managing university culture: an analysis of the relationship between institutional culture and management approaches, *Higher Education*, **32** (1), pp 41–61

Staff Educational Development Association (SEDA) (1998) Response to initial consultation on Booth Report, www.seda.demon.co.uk/index.html

Steneck, N H (1994) Ethics and the aims of universities in historical perspective, in *An Ethical Education: Community and morality in the multicultural university*, ed M N S Sellers, pp 9–20, Berg, Oxford

Sternberg, R J (1994) PRSVL: an integrative framework for understanding mind in context, in *Mind in Context: Interactionist perspectives on human intelligence*, ed R J Sternberg and R K Wagner, Cambridge University Press, Cambridge

Tann, S (1993) Eliciting student teachers' personal theories, in *Conceptualising Reflection in Teacher Development*, ed J Calderhead and P Gates, Falmer, London

Taylor, I (1997) *Developing Learning in Professional Education: Partnerships for practice*, SRHE/Open University Press, Buckingham

Taylor, K L (1993) The role of scholarship in university teaching, *Canadian Journal of Higher Education*, xxiii-3, pp 64–79

Terenzini, P T and Pascarella, E T (1994) Living with myths: undergraduate education in America, *Change*, January/February, pp 28–32

Tierney, W G (1988) Organisational culture in higher education: defining the essentials, *Journal of Higher Education*, **59** (1), pp 2–21

Tuxworth, E (1989) Competence based education and training: background and origins, in *Competency Based Education and Training*, ed J Burke, Flamer Press, Lewes

UKCC (2000) *Standards for Nursing, Midwifery and Health Visiting*, UKCC, London

Walker, M (1998) Response III: identities and contexts, in What does it mean to be an academic? A colloquium, ed J Nixon *et al*, *Teaching in Higher Education*, **3** (3), pp 277–98

Watkins, J and Drury, L (1994) *Positioning for the Unknown: Career development for professionals in the 90s*, Department of CE, University of Bristol, Bristol

Watson, D and Taylor, R (1998) *Lifelong Learning and the University: A post-Dearing agenda*, Falmer, London

Westergraad, J (1991) Scholarship, research and teaching: a view from the social sciences, *Studies in Higher Education*, **16**, pp 23–28

Winter, R (1995) The university of life plc: the 'industrialisation' of higher education?, in *Academic Work: The changing labour process in higher education*, ed J Smyth, pp 129–43, SRHE/Open University Press, Buckingham

Wittrock, M (1986) Students' thought processes, in *Handbook of Research on Teaching*, ed M Wittrock, Macmillan, New York

Wright, J (1997) The professoriate: relentless rise or decline and fall?, in *Uneasy Chairs: Life as a professor*, ed J Richards, pp 1–7, Unit for Innovation in Higher Education, Lancaster University, Lancaster

Further reading

Ashcroft, K and Foreman-Peck, K (1994) *Managing Teaching and Learning in Further and Higher Education*, Falmer Press, London

Avis, J et al (1996) *Knowledge and Nationhood*, Cassell, London

Barnett, R (ed) (1994) *Academic Community: Disclosure or discord?*, Jessica Kingsley, London

Becher, T and Kogan, M (1992) *Process and Structure in Higher Education*, Routledge, London

Bines, H and Watson, D (1992) *Developing Professional Education*, SRHE/Open University Press, Buckingham

Boud, D (1990) Assessment and the promotion of academic values, *Studies in Higher Education*, **15** (1), pp 101–13

Brookfield, S (1993) Through the lens of learning: how the visceral experience of learning reframes teaching, in *Using Experience for Learning*, ed D Boud, R Cohen and D Walker, Open University Press, Buckingham

Brookfield, S (1995) *Becoming a Critically Reflective Teacher*, Jossey-Bass, San Francisco, CA

Burrage, M and Torstendahl, R (1990) *Professions in Theory and History*, Sage, London

Cervero, R M (1988) *Effective Continuing Education for Professionals*, Jossey-Bass, London

Cross, K P and Steadman, M H (1996) *Classroom Research: Implementing the scholarship of teaching*, Jossey-Bass, San Francisco, CA

Eraut, M (1992) Developing the knowledge base: a process perspective on professional education, in *Learning to Effect*, ed R Barnett, SRHE/Open University Press, Buckingham

Garrett, D and Holmes, R (1995) Research and teaching: a symbiotic relationship, in *Research, Teaching and Learning in Higher Education*, ed B Smith and S Brown, Kogan Page, London

Gibbs, G (1995) Research into student learning, in *Research, Teaching and Learning in Higher Education*, ed B Smith and S Brown, Kogan Page, London

Goodlad, S (ed) (1994) *Education for the Professions*, SRHE and NFER-Wilson, Bucks

Graham, J (1998) From new right to new deal: nationalism, globalisation and the regulation of teacher professionalism, *Journal of In-Service Education*, **24** (1), pp 9–29

Gregory, K J (1998) Priorities in research into learning and teaching in higher education: a management perspective, SRHE/CVCP seminar, http://www.srhe.ac.uk/cvcp984.htm

Groteleuschen, A D (1985) Assessing professionals' reasons for participating in continuing education, in *New Directions for CE*, no 27, *Problems and Prospects in CPE*, ed R M Cervero and C L Scamla, Jossey-Bass, San Francisco, CA

Halliday, J and Sodon, R (1998) Facilitating change in lecturers' understanding of learning, *Teaching in Higher Education*, **3** (1), pp 21–35

Hoyle, E and John, P (1995) *Professional Knowledge and Professional Practice*, Cassell, London

Knox, A B (1985) Adult learning and proficiency, in *Motivation and Adulthood*, ed D A Kleiber and M L Maehr, JAI Press, Greenwich, CT

Kugel, P (1993) How professions develop, *Studies in Higher Education*, **18** (3), pp 315–35

Larson, M S (1977) *The Rise of Professionalism*, University of California Press, Berkeley

Lupton, D (1999) *Risk and Sociocultural Theory*, Cambridge University Press, Cambridge

Mezirow, J (1983) A critical theory of adult learning and education, in *Adult Learning and Education: A reader*, ed M Tight, Croom Helm and OU Press, London

Nelson, W C (1981) *Removal of the Teacher Scholar*, Association of American Colleges, Washington, DC

Robbins, D (1993) The practical importance of Bourdieu's analyses of higher education, *Studies in Higher Education*, **18** (2), pp 151–71

Usher, R and Bryant, I (1989) *Adult Education in Theory, Practice and Research: The captive triangle*, Routledge, London

Watkins, J (1999) Educating professionals: the changing role of UK professional associations, *Journal of Education and Work*, **12** (1), pp 37–57

Wilkin, M (1996) *Initial Teacher Training: The dialogue of ideology and culture*, Falmer Press, London

Index